REA

D0900134

✓

Rhapsodies of a Repeat Offender

Other books by Wayne Koestenbaum

Ode to Anna Moffo and Other Poems

Double Talk:
The Erotics of Male Literary Collaboration

The Queen's Throat: Opera, Homosexuality,
and the Mystery of Desire

RHAPSODIES OF A REPEAT OFFENDER

poems

Wayne Koestenbaum

Persea Books   New York

"I'm Not in *Darling*," "The Sacred and the Profane," and "1970"
appeared in *The New Yorker*. Other poems in this collection
were originally published in *The American Poetry Review,
Boulevard, The Kenyon Review, The Paris Review,* and *The Yale
Review*.

Special thanks to Karen Braziller, Michael Braziller, Faith
Hornby Hamlin, Jacqueline Osherow, and Jeanne Schinto.

Persea Books, Inc.
60 Madison Avenue
New York, New York 10010

Library of Congress Cataloging-in-Publication Data

Koestenbaum, Wayne.
    Rhapsodies of a repeat offender : poems / Wayne
    Koestenbaum.
      p.   cm.
    ISBN 0-89255-200-X
    I. Title.
    PS3561.0349R47   1994
    811'.54—dc20   93-40192
                                                             CIP

Designed by Hh Design
Typeset in Linotype Bembo by Keystrokes, Lenox, Massachusetts

Manufactured in the United States of America
FIRST EDITION

for Steven Marchetti

✣ CONTENTS

ONE

❧ RHAPSODY

Long ago, before
the complicated
    universe
grew Copernican,

I tore my twenty-
dollar leather coat
    on a fence
and saw the ripped sleeve

as replica of the dog-eared dollar bill
    I mailed away for Gordon MacRae
glossies which arrived a year—or centuries—
    late, inducing a queasy delight.

I hid the photos
in my drawer, beside
    paste and paint—
dissimulation's

tools, useful if you are writing Chanukah
    poems with Elmer's glue on construction
paper and then dispersing golden glitter
    on the wet, nontoxic trace. Lessons

about Hawaiian
folklore disappear,
    but the leis
we sewed, while sitting

Indian-style, survive; so do the features
    of the delinquent, squint-eyed schemer.
The butt of a bad child is a holy place,
    sanctified by the paddle's notice.

I watched the wicked—
selected by dice
    or by straws—
endure the board's touch,

whacks like open fifths.
Octaves hurt the hand,
     but I love
octaves for hurting.

"The Brahms B-minor
Rhapsody is real!"
     my detail-
hungry teacher cried;

"You are playing a genuine concert piece!"
     The two F-sharps in the right hand
revolted, so I telephoned my teacher,
     at sunset, for surgical advice.

Was she baking pound
cake, or practicing?
     The stars blinked
through the smog curtain

like numbers on an electric-blanket dial.
     Did we occupy the same time zone?
Did we see the same constellations falter?
     "Thaw out," she said. "Think of Brahms, not Wayne."

Her homilies come
back like frankincense,
     a fine mist
making my body—

when I stare at it—
mine. The past is blank
     if I don't
visit it, and who

knows how to knock loudly enough on the door
     of the bolted, Lethean moment?
Our dance theme was "Summer Breeze," though it was held,
     like all good formals, in spring; a week

before its fanfare,
a pock-marked boy stole
     my answers.
Or did I show him

unrequested secrets? Practicing, I stopped
		and started so frequently I lost
the cerulean flow, the melody too
		note–by–note. Its pediment crumbled.

		On the Schumann score
		I wrote messages
				to myself—
		military codes

like "Renounce" or "Retreat," the teacher's stockinged
		calves so opalescent they rivaled
the scherzo, or the fog the scherzo summoned
		to blur a romance composed of flaws.

		I wanted to walk
		with my teacher's bow-
				legged mincing
		elegance, her cream

		hose exuding gloom
		and grace. I should have
				stayed in third
		grade discussing poi

		and pleasure with teachers
		whose penmanship curved,
				Minerva
		arc on the chalkboard's

		sea without a reef
		in sight . . . . But time passed,
				I grew up,
		I stopped yearning to

become Shirley Jones in *Carousel,* her breasts
		on the soundtrack album cover two
innocent mounds without intention, only
		aware of the jumper that hid them.

		I wanted to be
		Sophia Loren
				or just near
		the idea of her.

When I'm old I'll write
a novel about
          my parents
on their nuptial night

in Niagara
Falls, my stocky sire's
          German and
Spanish accent—who

could refuse to love
a refugee in
          baggy pants?
My body's changing

or eroding though I'm only thirty-one.
          I tried to write a frenzied novel
at twenty, telling all the stories at once,
          a perfume-atomizer version

of sequence: droplets.
No design rises
          from the dead
abandoned pages—

prose in a coma,
its breastbone shattered,
          trapped in my
bottom drawer's Garden

of Adonis, far
from nurse or companion—
          as if I
could be a different

writer than I am doomed to be forever,
          repeating these tales and no others.
The woman that I imagine with blond hair
          naked on the rug is a novel,

a saturating
omniscience who knows
          that I will
eternally make

infatuation
my one motivic
        principle—
as, in Baltimore's

historic zone, I
prayed the Washington
        Monument
obelisk might be

the Chartres I'd never seen: a spire, a *stretto,*
        where sixteenth-notes hurry, holding hands . . . .
In first grade I lied, claiming the ceramic cow
        bought at the Halloween carnival

was my brother's creation. The teacher looked
        at the beast's udders and read the tag:
"Made in Japan." Then, though sworn to secrecy
        at Burger Pit, where knowledge was spilled

like catsup, I told
the class, "My mother
        is pregnant."
Do you start above

the note, do you rotate the wrist, do you let
        the fingers slave alone? Is the trill
a subset of the kiss? And how does Mozart
        or Chopin enter the beehive brain's

minuscule chambers,
grace notes or sustained
        funeral
chords leading you through

rooms you haven't visited in nineteen years?
        I remember my "I Spy" briefcase,
TV tie-in product with secret camera.
        When I flipped a latch, the lens opened

to embalm a dour sky that looked like dated
        exposés of Party abuses.
Last night I dreamt I dipped my brush in purple
        pools skimmed by the singing thrush, and drew

lesions on the face
I have often kissed:
        then I woke
to a sky turning

unknown shades of amethyst out my window,
        and I thought, "I must write this effect
down before it departs." Meanwhile the color,
        or my attachment to it, faded.

In high school, I imagined a circle jerk
        based on Franck's D-minor Symphony—
we'd time our climax to match the music's crest.
        How could I solicit membership

        or convince the club
        to remain loyal
                when rival
        conceptions of how

to achieve communal ecstasy, postponed
        in my monastic life, were growing
like weeds in a sidewalk's cracks? I stared at these
        sweet isthmuses, as on the beach where

        my science-minded
        friend asked me to strip:
                I complied,
        and collected rocks,

        seductive when wet,
        dull when taken home
                for private
        uses—their sheen gone,

why did I like the stones enough to steal them?
        What if I could steal the very seat
my father occupied in a Caracas
        movie theater in 1940—

        the moment he knew
        he wanted to be
                involved with
        music of the spheres?

The harpsichord is a chore and a shadow,
      it has loves to pursue. I played it
one winter but never learned that I can't swell
      a tone by digging deeper, I can't

      depend on pressure
      for crescendo, but
           must dement
      the rhythm so it

stumbles, hesitates expressively, the line
      opening its heart in quick crotchets
but then wanly refusing to designate
      what it loves, as in those John Blow songs.

      My ear is still primed
      to hear and obey
          harmonies
      that never appear;

presences stay pure if I don't write them down.
      Last night a whirlwind entered my room
while I was mouthing dream vowels, the long "o"
      or "i" of a mind whose reveries

are a wallflower's, and when the alarm rang
      suddenly the verb "exhume" appeared
with perfume adhering to its hem, as if
      I'd disinterred a clue by moving

      like a waterfall
      ahead in time. How
          Homeric
      and like the nightly

      unraveling shroud
      of Penelope
          our secret
      boyfriend existence

seemed in the summer when we drove in our used
      car to Magnolia's seaside rocks
and almost bought, at a yard sale halfway home,
      a Depression goblet. That cracked cup

couldn't say why life
resembled a yard
     sale, what goods
I was bartering,

or why my mother
sang the very song
     I loved, "Oh,
What a Beautiful

Mornin'," in her high-school choir. Similitudes
     spoke to me at midnight, their ichor
rising to my bloodstream's surface, releasing
     pleasures from captivity: they roamed

my bedroom carpet
and beheld the wise
     turntable
and sullen speakers

wanting to be full of volume, without hiss.
     I wonder if Gordon MacRae showed
his body to Shirley Jones, if she conjured
     his face while she sang, if musical

stars appreciate
the nearness of men
     in small roles
like the reporter

or prop man I am fated to incarnate,
     untrained understudy, never used
but always waiting for the leading man's demise.
     What is the theater? What is the play?

A sinister ghost
decided the boy
     in second
grade, without a name,

would slowly lose his hair from unknown sickness
     and miss huge portions of the school year.
His older sister came to pick up homework:
     a ruse. He couldn't learn while dying.

Part of his small head
was shaved—the sick half.
        The other
hemisphere was lush

with curls that seemed Satanic. The class sent him
        a "get-well" card, signed by everyone.
We pinned his response to our bulletin board.
        The day he returned, he drooled; his head

        lagged to the left side.
        A creep yelled "Baldie!"
                at recess.
        Did Baldie cry? No:

he scratched the bully's fat face, where pustules gleamed—
        pirate rubies on the ocean floor.
Baldie died that week, and his tormentor's cold
        sores turned into acne, and acne

        into solitude
        and serenity,
                but I still
        haunt the school's blacktop

to watch the molten collision of Baldie
        and the bully, atoms exploding
in fission: the universe is beginning
        again, and Baldie is the big bang.

❧ PIANO LIFE

The Wish Department

Today I sightread the last
Schubert sonata: he wanders between keys: evasive

and elementary, his melodies
meander. Tipsy Schubert,

if I were to return to 1974 for a piano lesson,
would my teacher say, "You've ruined your life,"

or would she just say "hello,"
and with her faraway "hello"

would possibilities cluster around my feet like clouds above the Andes?
The last time I saw her, I lied: I unfurled

fraudulent plans for a piano future.
I wish I'd learned a Schubert sonata in college: no,

I can't cry "wolf" in the wish department,
I *do* wish I'd performed the Chopin waltzes

so I can't bluff and pretend I also wish I'd mastered Schubert—
but I wish I could imitate Schubert now:

he says what he means, says it again and again,
shifts to a distant key and disappears.

Panavision

At my grandfather's funeral
I recited Milton's "day-labor" sonnet.
My day-labor is late and huge, I'm playing
Schumann's arduous *Carnaval.*
A degree of mignon masculinity animates my fingers this morning,

Bastille Day. When Schumann wrote PAUSE
I paused, I stepped into the backyard
and watched the impatiens as if my gaze were Panavision;
I took all the bastards in, their
plenty, their bit-part fastidiousness, their sullenness—

the garden promenaded for me while Schumann paused!
I spun around and kissed the dogwood,
the mute dogwood heard me play *scènes mignonnes,* the dogwood
did not bloom, Parsifal, on my holy account,
the dogwood stayed fast in its unprocreative

season while I played the "Chopin" section of *Carnaval*
(Schumann imitating Chopin!) with unwonted flurry.
Now Steve hums its plaintive melody, and says,
"Play that haunting bit again." I've haunted
my boyfriend: my métier is thunder.

Pansies

In the year 1992
Lord this is one of the magnitudes that shook me:
I played for the third time
Mozart's twentieth Piano Concerto in D Minor.
Maybe I should have graduated to another concerto

but Lord I don't own other concertos.
Lord I didn't make terrible errors but I coveted
one note at cost to the entire phrase;
Lord I stopped whenever I flubbed, and returned to fix
the aggrieved moment.

Long ago, at an audition, a bald, eminent judge
whispered my future
in measured words I can't remember.
Lord what did the judge whisper?
What cure for faulty playing did he propose?

At my final lesson, my teacher suggested future repertoire:
"Try Liszt's Consolation in D-flat."
Twelve summers later, my pansies lean their faces toward the sun,
and I attempt the proffered Consolation.
Realistic pansies, where did you live, years ago, when I needed you?

Modern Detective

I bought a Cream record and an Iron Butterfly record, $3.99 each
at PayLess near the Norwegian

pastry aisle, near the detective magazine aisle,
four blocks from where Karen, child of divorce, lived.

We necked in overgrown grass. I've mentioned
this scene before but never the tumult of the dandelions.

I am "male," a common, parasitic word,
green as the lichen on the rock where Orpheus wept,

the lichen that watched while Orpheus endured his operation.
On Gay Pride Day, we visited John, whose KS is worse.

We sat beside a white-flowering bush and talked about fear of God.
I imply no sanctimoniousness.

Mercury's Sandal

What kind of sandal
did Mercury wear when he flew on his impossible errands

across the sky, bringing news from god to god?
I will remember this as a heavenly day even if

heaven is cut, fifty-fifty, with remorse.
Lord don't kill me before the waltzes end.

I look out the window to see parallel
patches of petunias and daisies flanking

a square of modest sod, and up
the fence a fatigued clematis climbs, its five

flowers nearly gone. The dedicatee
of this waltz is Madame la Baronne C. d'Ivry

and when I play it, I become Madame la Baronne C. d'Ivry.
I shouldn't preen, or maybe God will take away the drunkenness.

What do Chopin waltzes remind me of?
Movies I haven't seen,

life I am leading up to and life I am wasting,
fits of blindness and fits of sight . . . .

I used to play the opening notes as incense fumes
and now I treat them as humble arrows toward a cadence, and beyond.

Veronica's Handkerchief

In youth my lazy sperm couldn't reach the distant tissue
outstretched like Veronica's handkerchief

waiting for the martyred, austere splash.
When a local saint played Liszt's A-major Concerto I had the rash

effrontery to say, "With your technique, Debbie,
why not try something more musically rewarding,

like the Brahms D-minor Concerto?"
We stood in the green room, and my question, about to be ignored,

had a sick, replete thoroughness.
The sacred Saturday my mother helped me

write a book report, she shooed my girlfriend away:
gold hair trailed up the girlfriend's thighs,

I saw it when her peasant skirt accepted
the wind's invitation to swoosh and rise.

What did my teacher mean when she said
"You have the temperament for Chopin"

or more precisely when she said
"You have the temperament for Chopin's E-minor Concerto?"

Dinu Lipatti died at thirty-three, my age;
he played Chopin etudes, all of 'em, in public

at fifteen. Not enough mornings left until Calvary
to learn the Schumann Concerto correctly

and yet I'll devote an hour this morning to its melancholy pastures
because I believe that Schumann, my first love,

this late in the millennium
still has secrets to whisper in my ear.

Hydrangeas

"Don't be a gargoyle," the great Tzerko warned me
when I played Beethoven with shoulders hunched.

Tzerko studied with Schnabel, I studied (a few lessons, tops) with Tzerko;
does that make me a descendant of Artur Schnabel?

It's not hard to be some big shot's descendant.
Through my first, dearest teacher, I'm a descendant of Dame Myra Hess.

I sit on the "descendant of Myra Hess" throne when I try
to hide the piano's innate percussiveness.

As I write this, my dead friend Marc taps my shoulder.
Marc, I didn't see you for months before you died

but in your garden I whispered an improvised
agnostic prayer and then

spooned your ashes over sun-faded hydrangeas.
You wrote nine letters to your boyfriend, to be opened

posthumously. In the eighth, you said of me,
"He doesn't know too many secrets." Did you mean

I once knew too many secrets, but have divulged them all?
Or did you see me as a selfish, sheltered guest

who steered the subject far from your torment,
which you concealed, even when you could barely walk?

Marc, you also wrote, "Not surprisingly, more
comes out in his poems than in his conversation."

This simple thing I wish to do with my remaining life:
play the piano a little better each month, play

like a mini-master, not like Myra Hess
but like someone who studied with someone who studied with Myra Hess.

Après une Lecture du Dante

My poetry teacher, who solemnly cared for beauty
more than she cared for men,
taught me Dickinson, and then

on the asylum's lawn
hanged herself. Now I'm playing Lizst's unmasterable
"Après une Lecture du Dante" sonata.

In what circle of inferno
does my beloved poetry teacher wander, her Clara Bow hairdo
aureoled by flame-tipped icicles?

In bed, lights out, we open the shades
to see the summer lightning.
"What's the purpose of lightning?" I ask,

and Steve says, "Go to sleep."
Mercury is skipping across the sky.
Jubilant, he has a letter

to deliver. I must fall asleep
to receive the consolation
of its unending vellum.

❧ EROTIC COLLECTIBLES

1975

Sodden on her bed,
we discussed rubato.
I zoned her crotch, deemed it
my focal point, my zero

degree: hetero coitus
was an engraved
manuscript whose figurations
I would trace

with an apprentice's slavish,
inauthentic brush.
Under the Blue Nun's influence
we smooched; a waxen

indifference, like hypothermia,
overtook me—also
a poignant intimation
that my intermezzo-loving

friend, in her sincere wish
to seduce me, had become
a suicidal emblem I could love,
her skin Fragonard

pink. She said, "If a guy is gay
there's a glaze
in his eyes. He looks
through you, doesn't see you."

Enlightened, I made a list
of possibilities
I planned, in dreams, to pursue:
the chef, the tuner,

the harpsichordist, the man
whose instrument I didn't know—
he seemed a clown, or acrobat.
I saw this carnival

curiosity in the laundry room.
He wore a muscle
shirt, black tights. His talk
was fast arpeggio, punctuated

by cackles. My whites
spun in the wash,
and then I moved them to the dryer,
after the saltimbanque

had removed his louche, aeolian linen.

1976

Her slant wit woke
my slumbering bolshevism.
Vestal, I vowed
to devote my life to her.

We sat in a nook: a stream
dithered beside us,
and a lark-attracting meadow
bestowed its tall slips

of grasses on our truant vision.
We were cutting counterpoint,
skipping *Sinfonia Concertante*.
Stoned, we were alone

with our bewildering intricacies.
I was fey, tenderly
built, with a taste of delectable
rot around the foundations.

My eyes, shaped like goldfish,
communicated muteness.
High during *Women in Love,*
I mumbled a private

incoherent mantra under my breath
about our irredeemable
passion, and when the midnight
show ended, we stumbled

through the streets, admiring
the moon's background-
foreground problem: was the moon
a solid, ponderous

element, or was it a peephole
in the sky, symptom
of a vaster phosphorescence
in sheets and plains

beyond our failing system?
We drank Black Russians,
then lay on our dorm lounge
floor for the night's

remaining hour: my life,
which hadn't started,
flowed before me, and I tried
to catch a phrase

from its unrealized congerie
of incident and wish—
as if I could prevent
a single scene from unfolding

in its proper, fated fashion!
She made me a goodbye
ring, at summer's peak,
from stolen multicolored

telephone wire. I wore it
with a widow's fidelity.
My violet, my bohemian
girl, has vanished,

but she retains a primavera
magnificence of train
and brow: I can't forget
the long-distance call

when with giddy abruptness
she said, "I wrote my name
on my arm, with a razor!"—
as if I should salute

this daredevil attempt at permanent inscription.

1977

This is how I learned
arts of suction, how stars
and comets of ancient sway
fumbled for preeminence

in my still adolescent body:
at the library
I interrupted *Paradise Lost*
to use the lavatory.

Hole between the stalls afforded
a view of my first man:
the archetypal divinity
student. We walked

through unearthly foliage
to his neo-Bauhaus
fascist-era dorm.
Down went our pants.

He had only one ball.
What happened to the other,
ghost ball? I stayed
until dawn, came home with guy taste

in my mouth, wondered
if my straight bunkbed mate
would sense my new
uncomely fellatio aura.

Was I aglow?
Was I visibly fallen?
This night had been
necessity, not pastime.

Burning, I revisited the trick
one numinous evening.
"I've got spring fever," I said,
justifying perversion

with the comforting old saw.
I wore Lee overalls.
Swashbuckler, he undid them.
"Enfold me, Satan," I thought.

By day I snubbed him;
only at night could I admit
I wanted to lie
naked and hoovered in his bed.

He had no extra flesh;
I remember his Irish
spareness. Now
you may be dead, my ethereal

initiator, you who led me
through foliage.
Each gesture was an accident.
No mythic embroidery

surrounded us, only
the story I am telling now:
the last time I saw you
I was drifting in cowboy boots

through the immense white
mystery of Garden Street,
my Bartók score
within a gloved hand,

sun against the already
fallen snow so unnaturally bright
I thought I was walking
toward catharsis—

my trio rehearsal at the block's end.

1978

He worked at a gas station,
or wore a gas station
jersey—or I blew him
near a gas station.

I said, "Can we go to your
apartment?" He said no
with sudden terrified solemnity,
as if it were taboo

to confuse tea-room and home sex.
I crammed this blow
job into my busy schedule
because my shrink had said,

"Have as much sex as you want,"
so by God I'd better
take the prescription and wake
my listless "Lycidas"-

reading body! How did I find
my way into his stall,
and did he welcome
my brash entrance, did he growl

"Hey there, foxy"? Dingy
light poured onto my clean,
hypothetical groin.
For ten syrupy minutes

he was the man in my life.
He waited for me, he didn't
pack up his dick and leave
the premises the minute he came.

Courteous, he understood
laws of reciprocity
that govern even the most
casual encounters.

What is casual? I did not feel
casual. My heart beat
fast, as if this were an audition.
After the event, I walked

down Revere Street, past
his gas station, or, if I
am imagining his connection
to gas stations,

then I can't justify why I associate his
mouth and its accompaniments
with a still-life Mobil sign
at trolley's end, where the sea

resumes its fabled nearness to the sand.

1979

I took the cable car to Liberty Baths,
I joined its circus;
I met the zoological
daguerreotype of a muscleman

who ran the refreshment stand;
I met the roseate jock
who said, "Just think
of what's in you," meaning

his penis; I met the featureless,
alabaster mannequin
who lay on his pallet like a lost,
uncatalogued Rodin,

waiting for a caption; I met
several ghosts whose virtù
a cloud has swallowed.
Where, thirteen years later,

lives the tattoo artist with pierced nipples
and hyperbolic love
talk—an unfrocked priest,
a sailor, a thief?

We lay on a leased cot
for one suspended hour.
I told him my age—twenty—
and he expressed wild wonder

at all the sex ahead of me:
the riptides, the lagoons,
the violations, the afternoons
in thirteen-dollar cubicles on Broadway

a mile before it meets the magenta, polymorphous bay.

1980

Sedans cruised past our bench,
overrun with vines,
as if this were the backyard
scene of *Sunset Boulevard,*

checkered by mishap and design:
absolute darkness
and brightness, a Manichean night.
He was pre-med, I

was pre-nothing: empty,
I sought the stars
in any street tramp's eyes.
The flatterer glozed,

"You look like Sal Mineo."
He meant waif;
he meant the stoics.
He was lying, or drunk,

and I became his disciple.
Yet when this innocuous
boy in a blood-red bomber jacket
wanted, for one night only,

my body, wanted my companionship
or my semen, wanted me
to want to stroke his
particulars, I decided VD

was a good alibi.
I took the name of disease
in vain. I lied: "I think I have VD."
If I woke the next morning

to sores and strange discharges,
would it have served me right?
Through his jeans I sensed
size: glimmering fish-sway.

My recently cut hair
had borrowed a Roman seriousness.
"Who are you?" he said
to my marble head,

heavy on my shoulders.
Unattainable, shorn, I was
Antinoüs, the morally
compromised boy, the fiasco,

the miscalculation.
So far I'd slept with twenty men.
I wanted to reach fifty
by spring. I doubt

I ever made it to fifty,
unless you count brief, silent
trysts in which the passionate
parties don't speak or touch—

interstellar episodes,
unsigned, pagan;
for example, the mimed
romance that began

when, at a revival theater,
I absently traced
my index finger—semaphore—
along my cracked lips,

applying imaginary Max Factor.
It was January 1980—
the world was stealthily
moving into epidemic,

and I was innocently
writing about the separation
between "word" and "emotion"
in the early poetry

of Ezra Pound, a thesis due the Ides of March.

1980

I turned carnation in the dining hall.
An abstraction
had taken refuge in my March
complacence; here

was delft-ware skin, a peculiar curved
upper lip, and a minute scar,
as if Cupid has rested his quiver
there for an instant

before departing for the next star.
Days later, we torrid
Pierrots interlocked
at a slumber party.

I thought, "I have found
a boyfriend." The word "boyfriend"
blessed my sodomitic immersions.
Boylove was my bank cheque;

I bought, I towered, I gorged.
I gave my boyfriend
a tank top to mark our tenth
consecutive day of romance.

I practiced the *Wanderer* Fantasy.
I read Baudelaire.
I cut off most of my hair,
shellacked the rest.

I smoked clove cigarettes
and stockpiled orgasms.
I wish I'd kept a sex notebook
so I could now read

fables of my naïveté—
our tournaments and jousts,
two sweaty chests pressed together
so tightly that when

they separated, a suction
"pop" was soundtrack
for our new-minted gambol . . . .
I ate his eyes,

his promises. No one mentioned
death, it had not yet
been invented. When his grandfather
died in April, one month

into our feast, we took the subway
to Park Street, and then
I let him go, unaccompanied, to the wake
in Wellesley; it wasn't time

to make my scandalous appearance.
Off he rode, on the Green
Line, and I tripped gaily back
to our deathless dorm.

The air was poetry;
I hadn't yet written
a single line of verse.
My uncanny love

resembled sonorous homilies;
a cross between
hyperventilation and asphyxiation,
love was a sublime

disorder of the breath;
the lungs took in
too much, too much,
then not enough.

I was glad, at last, to be
fabulous. I wore red
hightops and rose to my full,
egregious height.

I tried new tricks with tongue
and hand. I learned
the basics, and some personal
variations. My hyacinth past

rises now from mist
like a dinosaur in a pop-up
book about the earth's
ecstatic origins—far

from tomorrow's tamely twirling game-room globe.

1992

One man's dick had the quaint
malleability of Gumby—
and a Cheops eminence.
It was a private

theatrical. I smiled
at the melodramatically
self-exposing man and he
smiled back—intimacy

via mirrors in the men's room!
I'd made a friend
amid the dream's bulrushes!
There was no temporality,

no progression, no drama:
only teeming, succulent sight.
The proffered dick
in question was, naturally,

my childhood friend's: Dougie's.
It had the same hotdog quiescence,
the same look of threat.
Meat-colored, it stiffened—

a revolutionary
Gorgon or papyrus, veined
and brought out of pants
with a sensation of surprise

attack and anti-climax.
So one acknowledged
the penis but also said goodbye
to it, ignored it, nourished

no reverence. These men
were postcards; they wore
an arty stillness.
My chest's short wiry hairs

never converged
to form a general picture.
My terse pectorals
had a breast look. In the hollow

between the mounds
a saint's medallion hung,
to ward off injury.
You understand that in the dream

I was a timorous youth,
no nimbleness informed
my sexual conduct.
Outside, time's cataract cascaded,

and the weird tiled eternity
of the basement, the dive,
continued, a travelogue
I can't transfigure.

This was my vision.
These were the exposures
that lit up my night.
I saw the naked men,

I was one of the troupe,
and now I am telling you
about their tendrils, anatomies, smiles.
My never-to-be-fathomed men come here

to unzip their pants
and show me their message,
their lullaby,
their ghost story—

whose haunted ending never shifts:

1970

in the dressingroom
of Venus Swim School,
a mossy, gothic darkness
canopied the slatted walls,

and chlorine-saturated
swimtrunks filled the shed
with a note of panic—
time running out—

the drawstring forever
lost in the gauze space
where jock-pouch joined the suit.
In this cove I waited

for my father to strip,
but he retreated into a booth's
obscurity, and changed,
aloof from my greedy surveillance.

Moral in the cabana,
self-protective, shy,
he refused to become
one of my erotic collectibles.

Maybe he saw my gleaming
voyeur eye, and resisted.
Maybe he didn't want
to pander to a pervert son.

Or maybe I saw
more than I remember seeing:
maybe the withheld
glossiness revealed itself,

and I—afraid to offend
the gods who govern sequence,
telescopes, and night—
retained the picture

by forgetting it.
That summer I had no
erotic thoughts, none
that I can now recall:

only nectar, and privet, and shadow.

❧ STAR VEHICLES

I'm Not in *Darling*

Bette Davis has no reason to be jealous of Michelangelo Antonioni
and yet when I slept over at her house, in the late nineteen-seventies,
she kept me up all night complaining about a formerly illustrious career.
How her words came out is more important than the words themselves.

"I'm not in *Zabriskie Point*. I'm not in *Blow-Up*.
I'm not in *L'Avventura*. I'm not in *Isadora*.
I'm not in *Georgy Girl*. I'm not in *Woodstock*.
I'm not in any great sixties epics.

"I'm not in *Darling*. I'm not in *Midnight Cowboy*.
I'm not in *Easy Rider*. I'm not in *Valley of the Dolls*.
Why didn't they give me the Garland/Hayward role
in *Valley*? Why didn't they film *The Love Machine* starring me?

"Why didn't they film *Every Night, Josephine!* starring me?
Why didn't they remake *I'll Cry Tomorrow* starring me?
Or redo *Mata Hari*? I'm a limitless god, like Apollo,
but certainly I'd have done remakes in my dotage.

"I'm not in *Morgan*. I'm not in *8½*.
Ignorant armies crash my party.
I'm the haunted Bette always in your thoughts.
I'd have done any part, had they asked. Had they asked."

And then I woke, and discovered myself in the act of speaking, slowly,
        methodically;
and from the cup of tea, ambiguous steam-clouds, like locusts, were issuing,
in which I could read the pattern of my future,
a wilderness stretching farther than the exiled eye could see.

The Sacred and the Profane

Sophia Loren, whose birthday, September twentieth, I share,
displayed naked breasts early in her screen career
but then, with clout, curtailed these compromising exhibitions.
Does she wince when she sees originary nude footage?

I hid Sophia's photo in my drawer beside a miniature Torah.
In the photo, she is topless; in the photo, time has a mimic
relation to time. She moves forward into the atmosphere
of which she is already the sterling, solitary constituent.

If the photo aroused me, the sensation of arousal was joined
to Egypt, to the bitter herb, to the afghan my mother knit,
to scented desert isles, and to Lesley Ann Warren
in *Cinderella* and *The Happiest Millionaire,* pomegranate sheet-music

to one of its hits purchased on Saratoga Avenue,
dividing line I crossed during torrential rain.
"Before you were born, boys played football on Saratoga Avenue,
now a dangerous thoroughfare," my mother said, commenting

on masculinity, diaspora, decadence,
and the nature of streets, which change names and functions,
just as boys turn into men and then into dead men,
and parsley—transformed by salt water—into tears, and stars

into all varieties of immortal, blurred concupiscence.
What was the name of the *Happiest Millionaire* hit?
Where is Lesley Ann Warren now? Where are the women
who wear Sophia Loren glasses? To what bounty do I remain blind?

Ida's Glove

Ida Lupino appeared on "This Is Your Life," one of her hands gloved.
Some prior mystery ruined the hand; she wears a glove to hide the flaw.
Her protegées rustle in the studio audience,
waiting to bear public witness to the star's *noir* greatness.

Ida owes me an explanation for her glove on "This Is Your Life."
Was the defect congenital or late-blooming? Was the hand paralyzed?
What undocumented malady justifies the glove on national TV?
"Hello, Ida Lupino, this is your life!"

I, too, had a life, most of it unextraordinary.
I will not trouble you with its detailed recapitulation.
Watching Ida on "This Is Your Life," I discover a place for my perplexity:
1956, when my mother was twenty-six, and I wasn't born, is still a cue ball
          poised for flight

on the past's green baize pool table, amid smoke and raillery
in the pool hall where I gamble away my life,
the pool hall of acedia, the pool hall of worthless fancy,
the pool hall of sacrilege and rise-and-fall.

In Ida's movies I see no enigmatic glove, no wounded hand.
Damage only appears belatedly, on "This Is Your Life."
Thus the program is not her career's flattering summation
but an extra, disastrous occasion, masked as joy.

Rita, Time, and Space

Rita Hayworth in *Tonight and Every Night* and *Affair in Trinidad*
looks like my fancy ladyfriend I privately nicknamed "Time-and-Space"
because after her husband went mad and emptied a revolver in the ceiling
she drove to Cape Cod murmuring, "I need time and space,

time and space." When Rita Hayworth, dancing, raises her arms,
I see her armpits, so early, so purged, so clean, so mute,
that the flesh, and the peripeteias concealed in my stare, have passé charm,
and seem opposed to gym, where limited-edition ephebes ritually removed

their jocks. Forgive my indiscretions. I say what I remember, nothing more.
Rita's stardom exceeds the silent era; she has the hurt audacity of sound.
Why does Rita Hayworth—a fizzling quality—make me wish
to stand tall as Dionysus, to become Dana Andrews in a uniform, to drape
          my arm

around a woman, and give up my earliest memories, my emptiness,
     my moxie?
Around the childhood block lived a quotidian Rita,
beautiful as Rita Hayworth. "Around the block" means on the other side
of the spirit, in the land of dahlias, where ranch houses were stark as lakes.

Rita threw a birthday party for her son Randy
and took us to the local amusement park, where, on the Ferris wheel,
I blanched, afraid of turning upside down, afraid of transubstantiation.
After the ride, Rita said, "You looked scared to death," and I replied, lying,

"No. It was a blast. Time and space exchanged places."
How weak and musical was my demur, my evasion!
I was ashamed to say, "Yes, Rita, I trembled, I almost lost my soul."
She stood on the ground, watching the godless boys rise on the wheel.

She watched my terror, and my later concealment of it.
I was backlit, like Billy Bigelow after death in *Carousel*
beholding his misfit daughter's exile from June revels;
I was returned from the dead, detached, to observe the anthropology of my
     own horror.

Behavior and Misbehavior

Raquel Welch appeared in my bedroom before the proper world began.
How did I align myself with the axis of her visitation?
Imitating the poster for her first vehicle, *One Million Years B.C.,*
I fashioned breasts by bunching paper towels in my shirt.

Alas, I was barred from seeing X-rated *Myra Breckinridge,* co-starring
     Rex Reed,
whose works and name were contained in the Rose Garden Public Library
up the hill, where cacti thrived, and the highway curled, and the sheer edge
beckoned—a precipice I often trespassed, after borrowing fairy tales.

Rex Reed is part of the Rose Garden complex;
so is Mae West, who hid her age, discovered Cary Grant,
and wrote *Goodness Had Nothing to Do with It,*
which mentions musclemen and Brooklyn, my mother's birthplace.

In a late section, an appendix on eternal youth,
Mae recommends rubbing coconut cream every night into your breasts.
In arts-and-crafts I built a Mae West replica from construction paper
and animated her hinged legs and arms across a painted landscape.

If I could choose my name anew, I'd choose Pierre,
a name connected to subtitled adulteries, as Roger Vadim
is connected to Brigitte Bardot, and Bardot to the Lord,
via her vehicle, *And God Created Woman*—treasured because I never saw it.

I discovered the invisibility of stardom when my friend with Broadway talent
and buckteeth and braces took me past the saws in Penney's,
past household appliances and couches, which adjoined nonpareils,
and turned me on to the significance of Mae West's hands

writing in the saloon air the traces of her unfathomable autobiography.
In the song I am always murmuring, you can learn
about Raquel Welch, dormancy, insubordination, and auras,
which have a dreamy habit of drifting off the body as if they wished to flee
        the earth.

Auras are part of the Rose Garden complex.
The Rose Garden complex includes a million blooms,
but who can trust a star to answer fan mail, or to remain
in the venerable arrondissement where she was born?

The Garbo Index

My dead friend Vito praised Garbo's last scene in *Queen Christina*—
the closeup uncomprehended gays stared into, seeking dissolution.
I remember Vito eating pizza at my table in the Village, 1986.
He removed the sausage nuggets, placed them at plate-side.

"I don't eat pork," he said: HIV-positive precautions.
He was watching his system, as we were watching our own systems,
and are, to this day, watching. The last time I saw Vito entirely well
he was wearing pearls on his bare chest, high tea, the Pines—

never my scene. Who co-stars in *Romance?* Can't ask Vito.
When he was alive, I never helped him very much,
and now he's beyond telephone—waiting with Garbo
by the schoolyard's huddled ailanthus; waiting for the fire drill to end.

Four new Passover questions. Am I a child or an adult?
Am I a creature of memory or of action?
If I knew I were to die tomorrow, would I phrase this question differently?
Is it valedictory to write about Vito, or is it vanity?

My life is small, formal, and walled, and around every vista
I contain, imagine black shutters, the limits that Garbo
decreed must flank the lens filming her face in closeup,
so she could see only the camera's eye, without distracting leading man and
 crew.

Her life, if indexed, would yield surprises,
as would any life, if indexed, if reprieved.
Sea glass, Garbo's collection of. Camellias, Garbo's paradisiacal.
Grotto, Garbo's imaginary. Ghost, Garbo's.

Once, Garbo was whispering secrets of performance
in a bandaged voice, and I was listening, and no toxins in the field
of vision arose to violate the soliloquy, unfolding
with the tranquillity of all final compositions.

Haunting Tune That Ends Too Soon

In the early years of plague, I knew a guy who died named Crawford:
William Crawford, in a tux. But this is not his poem.
This is Joan Crawford's poem, dressed, like a bungalow, with regrets,
with unpainted, storm-worn shingles, and a front door loose on its hinges.

I want to march in order, star by star, and mantle each star
with reverie, but the star and the reverie don't match,
and Joan's picture, above my bathroom sink, is eternally cold and flat and
 hopeful:
the look of a woman with treasures in store, like Liz in *National Velvet*.

Now I will tell you a story. Before I'd heard of Joan,
I peddled Christmas cards, and ventured on the ragged lawn around the
 block;
I disobeyed the sign, "Do Not Disturb: Daysleeper."
I was desperate to see the face of the day-fearing nurse.

I knocked, woke her, and said, "Would you like to buy a box of glittery
        cards?"
She handed me a fiver. Remember, her clumsy daughter had a crush on my
        brother,
and had given him a gyroscope. (He spun it a few times,
laughed, and then threw it away.) A macabre nimbus

mantled their fatherless house, as if the nurse worked nightshifts
because darkness confirmed her alchemic nature.
The day I knocked, her face was yellow, and she spoke with difficulty,
        conscious
of invisible persecution. I felt guilty, a year later,

when she turned a deeper yellow, and died, in her thirties.
I felt I'd murdered her, the only magical denizen
of an unmagical town. She died on Driftwood Drive, the street of spiraling
liebestod, the street of hallucination, where a solitary modern apartment
        complex

loomed with the menace of the unwed and the unforeshadowed,
and flame-bright bushes between the buildings
promised that the nearby public library
held secrets of nuclear contamination, and our immunity from it.

On the way home I passed a ravine.
Time stopped. In the ravine I look now to see
Joan, ideal as a Piero fresco, before me, as if she were emerging
from the womb of the undead daysleeper, and my complicity with her
        martyrdom.

Joan and I slowdanced. The ballroom floor swooned.
She forgave my homo sins. All homo tangibles fell away in the sweet pressure
of her starlet arm, Joan and I slowdancing, torsos joined;
Joan whispered in my ear, she forgave, and her muttered word

"homo" had mist around it, as if marked by a sweet-tempered, revocable
        pestilence.
She revoked it; took it—the "homo"—back; then the spectators left, and
        Joan and I
twirled in the ballroom's center (Dorothy Kirsten is now dead
but Dorothy Kirsten was singing, live, into the microphone,

lasciatemi seguire il mio destino), and the ceiling
opened so we could see Astaire starlight shining down—
we couldn't tell whether stars were on the floor or in the sky where stars
      belong;
Joan and I danced around the sixteenth of September 1930 (my mother's
      birthdate)

or the sixth of April 1928 (my father's birthdate);
Joan erased my homo future, and married it,
so I was sealed off from my nature and enclosed by it,
observing its festivals, and yet in solidarity with no principle

beyond Joan Crawford's resemblance to Deborah Kerr
and other Biblical priestesses and pedagogues—I mean the scene in *King and I*
("Shall We Dance?") where Deborah's hoopskirt has the peacock ambition of
      fanning out,
especially on the soundtrack album cover, where imperial satin reigns.

I have secret scars in places you'll never see:
scar on the verb, scar on the participle, scar on the clause,
scar on the alphabet, scar on the flash card, scar on the multiple-choice quiz
on California's cluttered history, which I studied, and studied, and then

forgot—forgot the cravings of the Donner Party,
the adobe of the visited mission, the reason why we were named the
      Golden State,
and the reason why the poppy, flower of forgetfulness, was our natural
      product,
illegal to pick, though it grew unfettered along the tragic roads.

Two

⚜ RHAPSODY

I

What if I were not

*

yet alive but hovered on the verge of life — what if the words "what if" signaled

*

death, and the asterisk in the middle of the page

*

shattered my body into atoms?

*

What if poetry were dead and all I possessed were this

*

urge to explode,

*

the asterisk my navel opening to the world

*

because I am not yet born, my sex unknown: will you decide my sex

*

for me, transfix this fluid pouring out — will you

*

determine (and limit) the phosphorescence?

*

All I've ever sought is a more extreme way to be nude,

*

to suffer

*

away from home forever, an orphan in the world —

*

Occasionally this velocity will

*

induce nausea, as if my mother were standing over my grave —

*

I will punctuate later, I promise,

*

but for now let the leap

*

be musical — let at last Chopin's Berceuse enter my bloodstream

*

as if I were careening

*

past captivity's star –

*

Though in a secret part of my body I am authoritarian,

*

the only music that will ever

*

entrance me is unrestricted –

*

There is no use clinging to the descriptive or the morose – so much happened
    so long ago but dare I

*

submit to the stratosphere's final

*

elucidating detonation, to

*

explode and expose everything I am and contain, and not be content

*

with smallness?

*

Impossible in 1991 not to demand escape from the already-known,

*

not to rush across the page like Venus in its

*

ecstatic transit toward what you, too, want, if you could

*

frame the question –

*

if you could frame the desire we share, which is to

*

float, amber and burnished, above the sentence: no apostrophe

*

will carry me forward toward you, friend, atmosphere,

*

you the line I draw across the page and sky to find

*

myself, a child again, stranded

*

at the crossroads of what I know and what

*

I can't refuse any longer, evidence so huge and saturnine
            *
you, too, must stand in its path and be brightened by it —
            *
The tyrant has vanished, and around me
            *
stretches the infinite space of choice, so I wake in the morning
            *
and ask the sheets, "Am I in trouble?" — and the void
            *
answers, "Who are you, and what is trouble?" and the closet door on its
            solitary hinge
            *
breathes — as if my life were a book no one had sold or
            *
solicited, a book with broken spine, brittle pages
            *
crumbling, type blurred and edgeless —
            *
The evening I watched *Carousel* and wept at Shirley Jones
            *
because her breasts had already been seen and spoken for
            *
is irretrievable —
            *
I want to accelerate but I am afraid
            *
to become my father or mother — impossible parabolas — not
            *
feasible within the logarithm of Wayne, the only seizure I know —
            *
One need not be polite or introduce the matter of AIDS
            *
decorously, one can say "AIDS" many times and no one will complain —
            *
but what subtler prognostications are foreshortened I cannot judge or say —
            *
Place your life sideways and ask if it hurts —
            *
A body torn and bleeding, a body with AIDS, a body with
            *
innumerable spreading cancers

*

is still a body, and where its limits are set and (will you seduce them?) arraigned,
*

more of moment begins to speak, at the fringe of where I have usually spoken –
*

A wild universe contiguous with mine
*

has been lashing me for thirty-two years and until today I never listened –
*

How long, if stretched on the rack, does the body last
*

and how can you know a *declaration of limit*
*

from ecstasy?
*

Nobody said I wasn't well-meaning though sometimes
*

hostile and malproportioned and working tirelessly to circumvent
*

reason's proven pathways –
*

At the dinner table I have been mimicking people I detest
*

and discovering (childhood fear) that my face is stuck
*

in the physiognomy of the foe I'm imitating,
*

a face slack with grief and terror, mine
*

yesterday, when I was walking to school, and I saw, in a bush,
*

a sudden poem forming around the prickly berries, as if thorns had the gift of tongues –
*

Though we usually think pain moves forward like a cortège, in fact
*

its progress through the body
*

is S-shaped, a sly kouros –
*

All I revere has died and I hang, listless, on experience's hem,

*

as if, in childhood, near Gilroy's artichoke stands, my father's Rambler
broke down

*

and my mother began to cry

*

and my brother wet his slacks

*

and only I remained immobile and serene, sane and yet

*

discomposed from within, as if a hand with wooden spoon had never,
since my birth,

*

stopped stirring, nor had the gruel of consciousness congealed or added up
to much

*

through three decades of toil

*

and here at the edge of Gilroy, at the edge of the poem, car stalled, mother
asleep –

*

her open mouth a gauze, a frenzy –

*

the back of my father's head

*

martial, adequate, sulphurous,

*

and Wayne staring out into space, toward the limit

*

and finding there a bird whose name he doesn't know –

*

a bird that flies in circles

*

and whose mating cry is a silent kiss in the girlfriend's house, the party
room –

*

If I pick up the phone and find

*

you breathing heavily at the other end

*

then will I –

*

indubitable smudge in a torn-up photograph –

*

die or will I rise to a new, blessed, gesticulating height?

*

A mistake, to think you are

*

separate from the rhapsody, from the strained voice soaring toward the
      cadence –

*

This F-natural higher than the swallow goes

*

is not, dear heart, describable –

*

Soon I must confess specific things that have befallen me or else I will die or
      collapse

*

with grief –

*

I have written several poems and made many phone calls but never until now
      have I tried to describe the speed

*

of sorrow when it flies across the page and leaves no trace –

*

II

I alone among the living

*

can tell you about this particular experience I am having –

*

This morning I walked to the corner and posted a letter

*

and marveled at the marigold by the mailbox –

*

Where in China has my father, on his travels, wandered?

*

The traffic between father

*

and son is abyssal and

*

I remember my father skipping spaces when he wrote on yellow lined legal
    pads and
*

saying it is "illiterate" to cramp yourself on the page, hence
*

he believed in taking up the whole pad with his sprawl, handwriting
*

learned between the wars
*

or handwriting as a fact of war –
*

the very ammunition –
*

page after page contaminated with the commodity of my father's writing
*

and I cowering in the corner watching the arabesques of his math problems
*

correctionless, austere – O I tell you his equations were angelic
*

and no one dared starve them to see if they'd ascend –
*

My mother checked my spelling –
*

did she find it faultless?
*

I have sloughed off irony and dishonesty
*

though always in honesty's maw
*

deceit, a serpent, eats away the pith –
*

I want to move left to right with the swiftness of a repeat offender
*

and I want to be concrete again, as if concreteness
*

were a stuffed animal or replacement
*

object – fetish – to fend off night
*

owls and obelisks shadowing the child's Babylon, dreams
*

and broken bedtime promises ("I pray to God

*

that my mother and father live forever") –

*

I have been nursing vengeance schemes, as in *Rigoletto,*

*

since birth, which happened yesterday when I decided

*

I wanted to *be* the rhapsody, not merely pen it –

*

Since life is short I must immediately declaim and not postpone –

*

I haven't tested for HIV and I guess I would test

*

negative yet it is a crime to avoid diagnosis

*

since my conduct has not been clean –

*

All my life I have spoken meekly and suddenly

*

I learn that a sentence is a house whose glass roof admits the sky –

*

This is the ocean,

*

no substitutions, the thing itself,

*

and yet I am always sadly removed from experience, I stare at it through the
weft

*

of words, like the girl with webs between her fingers,

*

and yet no one teased, because her brother

*

was "hard" and thus kept at bay the Furies –

*

Teresa, Denise, Charleen –

*

Though every morning I wake and feel a slow tear travel down my cheek,
seeking

*

my mouth's Gibraltar,

*

I usually dismiss these tears as allergies
*
or the eye's natural watering process
*
but these liquefactions are accompanied by nostalgia –
*
gloom of knowing I have made mistakes and am still making them –
*
My last name is longer than anyone's and therefore so are my lines –
*
When I read this aloud I will snap my fingers like Carmen's castanets at the
    asterisks and halt –
*
snap –
*
like the camera's shutter
*
or in *Tango Palace* when Isidore the androgynous clown
*
at whim throws down a playing card
*
to signal syncopation,
*
heartbeat, or Horatian indecision –
*
The point is not to create some object but to render
*
time for you or (since you are I) to remain open to what
*
occurs as I begin to break
*
the covenant – I give you meditations on the mirror
*
and those meditations *become* the mirror
*
in which you stare and see
*
spectacles, eccentric narrow face, no cheekbone definition –
*
Bruce of Los Angeles captures what I like best in the human form
*
which is its nudity

*

substituting for consciousness and Aristotelian unities –
*

Because I am five foot five and one-half inches tall
*

I spiral upward like genie-smoke – "reality" the roof
*

my spirit curls against, a question mark –
*

In the pool I imagine breaking lane decorum and stripping the trunks off
*

the history student whose briefs reveal an exceptional stretch of loin –
*

Nothing would be gained by this conduct
*

except nudism, my only goal – or, beyond nudism, dance,
*

the one gesture I have always forbidden myself –
*

I just erased the word "remember"
*

or its first two syllables, "remem" –
*

Strange word, REMEM – in it do you see your fate?
*

The left margin is bound to my veins and the right
*

stretches to infinity, or my knuckles,
*

but what if for a moment, a mute inglorious
*

moment,
*

I gave up the velocity
*

and began to write at the customary pace,
*

decided to limit the line, to reinterpret
*

the left margin
*

as salvation? I can't stop

*

remembering pants pulled down to the knees and paddle raised in third grade

*

over the delinquent fat boil-marked butt of Bobby

*

whose penis looked like soggy Wonder bread –

*

I stared at it curiously –

*

"My chance to see a live penis!" –

*

Eden no longer interests me,

*

only speed, and the push outward from the pole of what you've called
    yourself until today –

*

I don't want to imitate myself

*

nor am I truly a self –

*

I stayed a virgin for eighteen years, and am still virginal,

*

recalcitrant, wary of huge experiences – I dislike being penetrated

*

by the new –

*

If there were to be a clearing in this chaos

*

what behavior would you demand of that oasis?

*

Today my face "wears" a hunted look, I try to smile

*

which effects no rejuvenation –

*

If I were a singer I'd have long ago quit singing

*

just as I quit trumpet and piano

*

but I can't quit writing, it is all I know –

*

Rhapsody, I didn't mean to kill you, I wanted you

*

to sit up straight and behave and tell your stories
*
in rhythm, coherently, with pauses for propagandistic pathos,
*
but instead you just
*
stopped –
*
Anything I love turns into a vise,
*
like the future, which I must, for your sake and mine, continue to trust –
*
I remember letting my baby brother crawl in bed with me and maybe I had
a hard-on
*
though I never touched him sexually –
*
He pulled my bangs and said "curly hair" as a taunt
*
or love-call
*
and in the car I said "Bing cherry!" which made him break up with laughter
*
as we drove past orchards now chopped down –
*

III

O for the inspiration to speak without error or apology!
*
I have lived through fifth grade and fourth and third –
*
I have gone backward and survived the trip
*
into the nether dark –
*
You who are listening, have you traveled there
*
and beheld the colossal space where nothing coheres or illumines?
*

I thought ill of these sentences when I was in the pool but aboveground I do
    not regret the swift
        *
heedless execution or the irreducible memories that recur and mar this
    Tuesday afternoon
        *
May 1991, the sun aware of its limitations, yet willing to shine
        *
on plant kingdom and on Wayne's house and on the house across the street –
        *
A second interpretation
        *
falls like hat-brim shadow over my mother's face
        *
and these terraced
        *
exclamations become steps on a porch leading to the back door
        *
open because it is May and sun floods the kitchen and makes the dust falling
    in columns
        *
a slow, sullen apotheosis, the sort
        *
you pray for and never achieve –
        *
Who cares about poems? I only want
        *
speech to tumble out of my mouth –
        *
None of these flawed statements
        *
expresses who I am
        *
but together they form a window frame through which you,
        *
if you cared, could peer tonight, and see my mournful face beam out –
        *
Cantors have long been my ideal, I want this plaintively
        *
to enter you and make you ask whose funeral it is –
        *
It is the funeral for my ambition and my youth,

    *
my cheerfulness, my hauteur,
    *
my belief in mother and father –
    *
My thirst is uncontrollable and lasting, it returns no matter how much
    I drink, which means
    *
I am critical of fountains
    *
I am critical of sources
    *
I do not believe in Ponce de León –
    *
but that judgment does not illuminate the precipice
    *
of this particular
    *
sentence which plunges through me and asks its own irreversible questions,
    *
each a whirring instant I can't discharge or refuse –
    *
I need to accomplish my childhood fantasy of becoming Mary Poppins and
    soaring
    *
above the school macadam,
    *
above Mary Ann and Pam and Mrs. Nigh, above distance
    *
and term papers, the appearance of sin and its actuality,
    *
above masturbation as an event in the future and a staple of today,
    *
above sawdust and pull-up bars, Boy Scouts and Youth Symphony,
    certificates
    *
and friendship, above *Carousel* and *Oklahoma!* and *The King and I*
    *
and the Saratoga Theater in which these films, revivals, were showing
    *
so indelibly that I have been saving for two years the words
    *

Saratoga Theater
*
as if the dreary and fantastic elements of that far-off time would flood the page
*
if I released those syllables –
*
I am sad about the nonexplosive aspects of my life –
*
my docility and decorum, my tendency to bow and toady –
*
all the mellifluent elements of my personality make me nauseated
*
because at heart I remain a firecracker – a "one-man firecracker committee"
    I called myself
*
on Christopher Street when I was buying a flowered bathing brief
*
and a belt so wide and inappropriate I will wear it for the rest of my life –
*
I flow and flow and never end, no rock falls in my stream to stop me –
*
the utterance glides out so gelatinously that the line
*
or the illusion of naturalness enrobing it
*
forgives the sentiment and its velocity, makes of speed
*
a ceremonial gesture, like a minion's noncommittal, unrehearsed bow –
*
I am saying "Sorry!" to unpleasant higher powers
*
seated in my head as if in graduation bleachers under the June glare,
    loudspeakers
*
crackling "You'll Never Walk Alone" which is already proved a lie,
    I have been
*
walking alone for a decade –
*
If I were a more considered soul I would have separated the composition
*
into several days, each day

*

adding a page, so that by summer's end

*

I would have a stack of aphorisms, reflections

*

on consciousness as I have endured it,

*

but instead, I rushed it all into the typewriter as if I were wounded, and
    typing

*

staunched the blood –

*

Do you excuse the incoherence

*

or even the gesture of asking such a question in the middle of what should be
    a plausible narrative

*

of my life rather than my life itself, dragonfly smashed on the page?

*

Nothing thrills me more than the swelling moment and then, following it,
    like a lady-in-waiting,

*

the obedient moment,

*

admiring, a tad mournful,

*

because my soul is split between the meek and the mercenary,

*

patience and impatience, the command and the fluttering acquiescence, like
    the thrilled

*

throat on the verge of a cry so bellowing no one, except myself, receives it,

*

unless you find in the exclamation's blueprint

*

the reverberation

*

of an intention, though no intention (just efflorescence)

*

precedes its minnow-quick execution –

*

I have been reading about singing for nine months and after this gestation

*

I am ready, at last, to open my mouth and let the air

*

vibrate in my mask's bones and mucous chambers –

*

I sang outside the bathroom and felt alive for the first time since sixteen –

*

did I feel alive then, or embalmed?

*

I want to be documentary, to mention the euonymus, pachysandra, and
impatiens

*

Steve planted, and the day-lilies we found waiting –

*

innocent, expectant shreds of a former yard

*

we trust will revive and shower us with petals –

*

A nameless nondescript bush has rewarded our complaisance with
mysterious yellow buds

*

too humble to call wild roses –

*

call them phantoms, echoes of the chrysanthemums

*

I gave Steve in 1980 because their pom-pom straightforwardness reminded
me of his jaunty, clean, yellow windbreaker

*

as if he would never commit a crime or genuflect to a fallible god –

*

I am growing sentimental

*

and the point is not, this time, memory,

*

but excavation into what has not yet occurred, nostalgia's

*

antithesis – tunneling into the future – probing

*

the instant at the edge of this sentence, the unclaimed hour

*

that will begin when I finally put a stop to this

*

exuberance and shamelessness −

*

Do I resemble a professor of divinity?

*

Sometimes I feel so spiritual and morose

*

I wonder if I have a second vocation awaiting me

*

as counselor to the fallen and sick, as dispenser of platitudes and comfrey −

*

My soul's a flawed stepladder −

*

I want to climb upward and my only rungs are words and my wish to plunge

*

ahead, blindfolded and belligerent, into the uncharted and gregarious

*

tomorrow − I mean

*

I believe that in the future I will be more talkative rather than less,

*

and what I become will define who I have been,

*

which we will call a *lie*

*

like the childhood photograph in which I have a Band-aid on my cheek −

*

The wound and its disguise

*

make me provisionally (in the future tense) myself −

*

I don't remember the nature of the wound

*

or the texture of the Band-aid

*

or the reason my shirt is untucked and my bottom lip juts out,

*

but I remember − tangent to that driveway, that sunshine − the chewed-up

*

remnant piece of graham cracker stuck behind a tooth

*

and then spit out and staining the crisp oversized page

*

of a children's picture book about wandering, uncaged animals —

    *

and I remember the graham-cracker mush, decomposed and vivid,

    *

as *more* than a stain — as

    *

introspection — as

    *

periphery that will not be named today, nor was its nature understood then —

    *

nor were center and periphery

    *

part of my soul's vocabulary,

    *

prone as I was to staying put on the driveway and never venturing further —

    *

but why don't I remember how sunny it used to be or why don't I remember
enjoying that light

    *

as the eternity and volubility it might have been — as source

    *

of every foment I could wish for, even before I had reached the wishing age?

    *

IV

Well, I've decided one important thing —

    *

I am still addicted to syntax —

    *

Last night we saw John who has

    *

a KS spot on his arm which he is not afraid to display

    *

and I love him for loving *The Boy Friend* more than any movie on earth —

    *

Each of us must nurse an inordinate, inexplicable love —

    *

Mine, today, is for the passage in *Andrea Chénier*

    *

when two male voices, a chorus posing as a crowd,

*

and the ghost of Maria Caniglia, already too old

*

to sing dulcetly,

*

promise that the French Revolution, a telephonic orgy, is about to happen

*

and that I am its cause and its beneficiary —

*

I don't want to explain an emotion, I want to paint a verbal ring

*

of posies or forget-me-nots around it, and let the circle

*

imply the sentiment, as a blouse in a closet suggests a body —

*

During a prior phase I sat in White Hen Pantry and over coffee

*

transcribed the ravings of bag ladies

*

into tercets and quatrains

*

as if thereby doing sanity a service

*

when in fact I was afraid to expose my *own* insanity —

*

I first heard my voice on a tape recorder in my brother's bedroom

*

and I said "The tape recorder

*

is broken" though I meant my spirit was broken —

*

Everything I say is split,

*

a shadow-consciousness observes and denounces the utterance before

*

it is completed

*

and my desire, through this untidy practice, is to ambush

*

he-who-foresees and set a place for him at the poem's table —

*

indeed, acknowledge that he is the sommelier

*

and without his purple vintage there would be no movement forward –
*

You'd think I'd given up crushes on women, since I declared myself exclusively
*

gay in print two years ago
*

but S. has the power
*

of touching a nether nerve I didn't know I owned –
*

some cell, remote from sex, that produces affinity
*

and chain reactions, like a foaming test tube
*

in my brother's toy chemistry set –
*

This sentence sleeps on the back of a *Contes Arabes* page –
*

woodcut of Aladdin surprised by the genie's
*

hoary emergence from a bottle on the sands –
*

Books are fun, they surprise their authors –
*

Last night I dreamt about Mark Strand
*

and the editor of *Genders* –
*

We were driving away, like convicts, from the castle of poetry
*

toward another kingdom –
*

Is this page the vehicle for that migration?
*

I detest fakery
*

but there is a tincture of insincerity in everything I write, even those honest
*

sentences that lift themselves, belly first, like a salamander,
*

off the page –
*
I want these words to go forward bashfully and assume, through
*
agglomerations I can't foresee, intangible
*
existence – only when amassed
*
can words creep, phalanx-like, toward an enemy –
*
What a waste of time if, instead of discovering
*
how I might render my mother's absences,
*
I substitute those lacerating caveats
*
with pale, pacific, puling sentiments
*
like "I don't know what my mother meant
*
that time she threw my brother's watch out the car window" –
*
"I never had a mother"
*
said Emily Dickinson –
*
I read Dickinson by my mother's side when I was a
*
sticky, solicitous, stuck-up sophomore –
*
Do I want to talk about my mother or would I rather have a glass of iced tea?
*
I dread the moment of chastising and diminishment –
*
not that I fear concision (I love to cut
*
sentences in half and see them shine)
*
but I am afraid of erasing the grounds, the surrounding suppositions, afraid, too,
*
of ratiocination –

*

I want to postpone the subject and make postponement
*

rewarding and jeweled –
*

"Andante" doesn't mean dull, it means walking tempo
*

and "prosaic" doesn't mean pedestrian, it means
*

sea-level, commensurate with the pavement –
*

On the way to the mailbox on the corner of Orange and Pearl
*

I realized my insignificance, and my locomotion
*

stopped, as it is stopping now –
*

Continue to probe this experience
*

I'm having, shimmer of distaste like oil (Della Robbia blue) in a rain puddle –
*

an experience I hardly understand, one
*

I've had before but it is new this time, faceted, unforgiving –
*

I am afraid of normalcy
*

subduing me –
*

I want to be red and lavender and puce –
*

to *be* the movies, not merely their recipient –
*

String quartet, please excavate my dissonances,
*

empty the lushness of each utterance and discover its brambles
*

coincident with my childhood, the driveway, the bush with red berries and
     wasp's nest,
*

rock at the pyracantha's base, rock on which I rested my leg, shorts
*

hiked above the knee – a shameful exposure since I disliked

*

the birthmark on my right thigh –

*

I skinned

*

my knee a thousand times on that red rock

*

which, rolled over, revealed a colony of worms –

*

The spectacle

*

proved I was alive and that there remained summits, escarpments

*

of sight beyond attainment –

*

Quartet Number Sixteen by Darius Milhaud is over

*

and here's a movement from an unfinished symphony,

*

perhaps Schubert – he's master of the unfinished –

*

but it sounds Russian, a work of mourning

*

as all unfinished objects are –

*

If you turn the page

*

too quickly you will see your death scene, already written, waiting to be
    performed –

*

This sounds like Bruckner's Seventh, background for Visconti's *Senso*

*

in which Alida Valli reminds me of

*

Vivien Leigh and my nascent heterosexuality –

*

I hate constriction, which is why I swim, but I count

*

my laps, and counting destroys the ecstasy,

*

makes it seem a foreknown,

*

violent verb, like *press* or *macerate* or *prick* –

*

I'm irresponsible to avoid the HIV test

*

and I imagine this long poem's climax

*

will be performance, not language – the act

*

of giving blood –

*

I once worried that Anna Moffo would sue me

*

for using her name and her story without permission

*

and now I realize that a suit

*

is a solicitation

*

as in *pursuit,* and that the relationship of *versus*

*

is a seesaw, plaintiff up, defendant down, then the positions reversed,

*

so I, by pursuing Anna, have sued her –

*

A Romance by Tchaikovsky divides the air –

*

Order and poise are distant eidolons

*

I've abandoned in quest of the immediate –

*

Every sentence, because it is a sentence, has been cooked,

*

but poesy's a Rubicon I'll not cross today –

*

If my shoulders are tense, then I have been false –

*

if relaxed, then I have been true, though honesty

*

itself is a flaw,

*

like putting the pedal down during one harmony and then gliding

      *

into a neighbor harmony,

      *

but carrying some of the prior overtones

      *

like feathers

      *

into the next key's universe –

      *

I've said too much, but I've stopped short before

      *

the awful majesty of the one

      *

thing truly worth saying –

      *

V

If I'm not careful I'll think I'm playing the octaves

      *

at the beginning of Chopin's E-minor Piano Concerto

      *

and that delusion will be a disaster

      *

unless I can reproduce the pleasure it gave me, at twenty, to know

      *

that Chopin was twenty when he composed the concerto –

      *

Why am I doomed to use so many words

      *

to describe my mundane rigor mortis and elation?

      *

If only I could steal back that moment when I walked across Cambridge
    Common,

      *

score to the Chopin E-minor under my arm!

      *

When I return from swimming, let music lull me back to the depth I fell into

      *

this morning, as into a lake during a lightning storm –

*

Adelina Patti, who looks like my sister and grandmother, stares from this
    page's verso
*

and asks what I am thinking, her gaze a flute –
*

I'd rather nap
*

than enter Ariadne's web of conjecture
*

and backward-tending contemplation –
*

Depletion depresses me – my glass of iced tea
*

was secretly water, and it is finished –
*

A guy's chest in the pool pushed me from poetry toward sex
*

and silent thought,
*

torso so hieroglyphed with hair, pectorals so developed
*

as he streamed like a porpoise through the water
*

that I wanted to crash into him, pleading myopia, and have the sensation,
    momentary,
*

of chest upon chest, mine less appealing than his but mine and nothing
    I can do
*

to change it, except swim –
*

Do I want to push the lines together
*

or let them stare at each other across the asterisk's fence?
*

Caught in candor
*

I harbor secrets I'll never know –
*

Two pigeons flying past my window beckon from the anterior life –
*

I dread this evening when, without antenna, our TV

*

won't receive *Un Ballo in Maschera* (broadcast at eight)

*

and while I stir broth into rice

*

I will condemn myself for self-indulgence and for pressing too hard

*

against narcissism, a frail subject –

*

The harp is slowing down, the flute is impatient

*

and I will hop downstairs vaguely disappointed that I've not reached

*

ecstasy this afternoon but have hit the soul's

*

ceiling, as if the prices in my head were fixed –

*

In the pool I vowed

*

to write about the space between my mind and the sky

*

which I will never reach and so can adequately and objectively

*

comment on its inaccessibility –

*

Words dwarf the life they depict

*

so loping downstairs I wrote these lines in my head

*

and felt comforted because the descent had already been described,

*

preventing me from occupying the lonely position

*

of one who commits an unprefigured act –

*

Possibly I'll carve away at the poem's carcass

*

until I'm left with one page about my life as an actor

*

in fourth grade and my crush on a girl named Chloe, seventeen, diagnosed

*

with leukemia – her recovery, and the discovery of misdiagnosis,
*
juxtaposed with my sister banging her hairbrush on my bedroom door
*
because I'd yelled an obscene word –
*
I will ignore the stiff sensation around my heart, contracting and contracting
*
so no expansion will ever right its balance –
*
Brokenhearted about next month's phone bill which will include today's
    impulse call
*
to a phone sex line and no one was on the line
*
so I spoke to space and treasured the sensation
*
of my voice bouncing off Sputnik
*
and landing in Providence and Phoenix
*
and returning to my receiver in New Haven, returning empty
*
but filled by my attention to its transit –
*
I crave the absence of reciprocation
*
a phone call brings to the moment
*
of orgasm – I crave the occasional stranger on the line who will tell me
*
something unpredictable like right now he is wetting his undershorts and
    do I mind? I say
*
of course not, go ahead (I won't have to clean the sheets) –
*
Erasure's an aphrodisiac –
*
Why don't I write about flowers? The impatiens at our fence's foot
*
give more joy than a single furtive orgasm on the phone
*

but I lack knowledge of genera,

*

and flowers only grow incarnate when named –

*

When I gaze out my window tonight while drinking vinho verde

*

one half-hour before Steve comes home and I dive

*

into the inebriating overture to *Luisa Miller* and my irremediable

*

distance from Anna Moffo whose picture tropically founders on the cover,
  a *mise en abîme*

*

(as if I'd placed two mirrors face to face

*

and stood between them and tried to see my soul),

*

then the impatiens, placid in May wind, unaware of the abstruse

*

fence depriving the neighbor of a view of them,

*

unaware of my remorseful, Sapphic glance,

*

only then are the impatiens

*

sacrificed to a spaciousness

*

I will never acutely name, but will spin around, a ballerina,

*

an automaton, for the rest of my life –

*

Only if I accost the scene hidden in the shadow

*

surrounding the turgid word I last wrote ("rue")

*

will the truer presence I shirked

*

flower into speech –

*

Why do I value this blossoming

*

at the expense of coherence and sociability?

*

When I use the word "ecstasy" do you take me seriously, or do you think I'm
 pulling your leg?

*

For a long time I thought my subject was homosexuality –

*

grim, medicinal word –

*

but I've always secretly been a mystic,

*

and I stumbled over sex as the stone obstructing mysticism's way –

*

VI

Tito Schipa please give me courage

*

to live in the middle of the mirror

*

and not measure what it means, morally, to see –

*

Last night, as I predicted, our TV couldn't handle the inscrutable waves

*

beaming *Un Ballo in Maschera* all over the world

*

and so sulkily I ate my grub at the kitchen table and felt like my mother
 because I'd just

*

bawled Steve out (I am selfish and cruel) for not having fixed the TV in time

*

to watch *Un Ballo* – as if the goddamned *Ballo* (supposedly an inferior
 production)

*

matters when placed beside domestic virtues –

*

Should I turn off the tape of Schipa and Galli-Curci singing the soppy duet
 from *Sonnambula*

*

that gives me shivers because it reminds me of when my grandmother was
 young

*
and my mother wasn't born,
*
a time before pompadours and
*
interviews with Bernard Baruch,
*
a time when my grandmother posed on a rock in Central Park with her hair shyly
*
bobbed, her face a cut cameo
*
I wear by carving this line?
*
I have no right to be sentimental about a grandmother I rarely call
*
but I have a right to be sentimental about sleepwalking
*
through my mind's Alpine chasms –
*
Tom the carpenter is here to replace the kitchen window with a larger one –
*
I favor wide windows, open to the mysterious view –
*
In "Verranno a te" from *Lucia,* soprano and tenor
*
float toward a horizon only they and Donizetti understand –
*
If you try to imitate it, you will fail –
*
No one but Galli-Curci, who's dead and always will be,
*
knows what waits beyond the horizon's edge –
*
Not even I who pretend to be an expert on edges
*
can fathom it –
*
"Io t'amo" –
*
They are always saying "I love you" –
*

Now Schipa is singing those silly Sicilian songs
*
only attractive if you imagine the villages in which they're set –
*
He begins the phrase in one moment and then
*
moves moltenly into the next,
*
whose bulb breaks into satiety, where I find nested
*
an arbor, sweetly scented,
*
which unfolds, a storm, and then, without premeditation, stops –
*
That is the rhythm I should be striving for
*
and I should never settle for the truncated, tormented line
*
nor for the day which refuses to be married to the next –
*
I'm in tenth grade beneath eucalyptus reading Elie Wiesel's novel with flame
on the cover
*
exempted from gym for a specious ear infection –
*
My mother was always willing to write me a gym excuse
*
during swimming season –
*
I examine the thought before it occurs and then sigh soundlessly
*
and refuse it entrance into my skull's hall –
*
I'd rather be in São Paulo
*
or in the Palermo summoned by Schipa's "ay-ay-ay" ballad
*
but a shadow is waiting to be spoken –
*
When my mother had fits
*
those moments of fit seemed ultimate – hell's Rockaway –

*

but a more sanguine sensation would dawn

*

and I'd forget the fit and learn again to love my mother though I'd vowed

*

not to invite her to my wedding —

*

I'll never have a wedding so I won't have the luxury of spurning her —

*

I'll spurn in subtler ways —

*

Now my favorite Schipa song, the most sentimental, is on —

*

"Pianefforte è notte,"

*

recorded in 1955, when he was sixty-six —

*

he sings flat, and I love the variant pitch —

*

If you don't share my taste

*

I'll have to hide

*

my listening ecstasies and protect Schipa, too,

*

from your scorn and judgment

*

as if he were the soft, dear part of myself no one has seen —

*

I'm sick of the strange, it's time to say the home facts —

*

I believe (credo)

*

in Satan and I believe that I *contain* Satan —

*

that is why I am polite and nice —

*

I must prove to you that I've conquered Satan —

*

If I acted as I desired, I'd smile all the time and radiate

*

a good cheer so brutal you'd want to run me out of town —

*

Schipa is singing "Una furtiva lagrima" –

*

Have I told you about the time I cried?

*

I'd seen *Carousel,* and a flood destroyed the fence, as if I weren't

*

wearing clothing

*

or muscles —

*

Silly pretext for tears – *Carousel* –

*

Did I revere the revolutions of barker Billy Bigelow's wheel

*

or his song to his unborn

*

son, "My Boy Bill"?

*

He won't be a sissy, sings Gordon MacRae,

*

and at an antique fair I saw an undersized Gordon MacRae record, *The Desert
Song* –

*

in-between issue, pressed when 33 rpm was new –

*

I didn't buy it, but I was glad to know that Gordon MacRae enjoyed a full
career before *Carousel* –

*

At my seventh birthday party (in pictures) I look like

*

a bite-sized Gordon MacRae –

*

I'd invited one boy, three girls, one of them Pam –

*

We had in common our love of the letter A –

*

Her mother sewed in a room filled with Chinese translations of *Simplicity* –

*

Pam played "Für Elise" and I thought I'd faint from joy –

*

She was my ideal of accomplishment –

      *

She became a translator for the UN –
      *

I too am a translator though I know only one language,
      *

static I sift into speculation –
      *

I would like to hollow out, with a spoon, my head's ripe pumpkin meat,
      *

so just the surface could smile at the world without distraction –
      *

The word "God" looks silly, unless you leave out the O and write "G-d"
      *

as my Orthodox students did, respectful of the word that can't be spelled –
      *

Distance, though lovely as all promontories are lovely,
      *

is separate from every place I have wanted to possess –
      *

In the mirror I notice my small gray bottom teeth –
      *

At least I lack cavities
      *

thanks to grammar school's yearly fluoride sessions –
      *

To test hearing, in a trailer, we wore earphones and listened
      *

to ominous air-raid wails
      *

descending to a pitch so low it meant holocaust –
      *

My father left Germany in 1936,
      *

a date that summons the memory of thirst
      *

because when he told me refugee confidences
      *

I was craving apple juice and coldly
      *

observing the checkerboard tile by Valley Fair Mall's drinking fountain,
      *

whose water I was terrified

*

and exhilarated to drink –

*

Have you ever lifted a load so heavy that your arm muscles shake?

*

I'm lifting such a load

*

by choice, so I can't complain, and I could lighten the texture and weight

*

by trampling each bursting exclamation, a grape,

*

but I love the sensation

*

of burden and strain

*

and I learned from my mother that strain could be pleasurable –

*

she strained just to get through the day

*

and I loved her for it –

*

My asymptotic consciousness will swell and push against what limit

*

as I wander around my past this afternoon?

*

Every time the orchestra in this Mozart concerto reaches a brass-tinged
climax

*

I feel the phone is ringing

*

and I must answer it –

*

What is dialing me up? Ecstasy –

*

I was a devotee of proper hand position

*

and the sensation of meaty key beneath the fingertip's pad –

*

I knew what a phrase's consummation might be, even if I could never direct it

*

toward its fate with my own hand –

*

I knew one or two tricks –

*

I could stress a chord's top note with the pinkie,

*

mask the inner voices, use shoulder's weight for a damp tone, or the

*

nail's underside

*

to make an incisive "ping" –

*

The glockenspiel's solo

*

drives through me like a saber

*

but I'll never be able to render it in words for you –

*

I need a *you*

*

to understand that I have experienced pleasure,

*

otherwise it no longer exists

*

and never existed –

*

Tom is sawing away the kitchen wall

*

and I've typed so violently, like the wild bunch,

*

that the element is breaking down –

*

This poem's covert purpose will have been the destruction of my
    instrument –

*

Sometimes I'd like to run into the woods and eat mescaline –

*

I am a waterfall who all its life has pretended to be a lily pad

*

or dandelion –

*

My smile is forced if you study it closely –

*

There are holes in my good manners and frivolity –

*

I'm not funereal, but I have lived on the dark side of the moment

*

ever since I read *Doctor Dolittle* and African fairy tales during naptime

*

while my mother vacuumed –

*

When I vacuum, I divide the room into imaginary squares

*

and then bomb one zone at a time –

*

How otherwise will I obliterate the whole room?

*

I was taught to believe in dirt's invisibility –

*

A carpet can be dirty even if to the naked eye

*

it appears clean –

*

Remember the phrase "dirty mind"? I had one –

*

I'd like the poem to be

*

so monstrous I skulk around its radius –

*

not because I wish the poem to be a skyscraper or a missile

*

but because, like a boy who wants to turn a trick so badly his pants are falling off,

*

I want to "turn" a poem – I want

*

the experience of lines building up in my head like lovers listed voraciously

*

in the old days when I wanted to sleep with fifty men just for the sake of the number fifty

*

and a knowledge of men's varied, cardinal flesh –

*

I don't want all these thoughts to live on *one* level, I want some to be prominent and others sheepish –

*

I want a hierarchy

    *

provided by looks and not by logic

    *

as if I were judging a beauty pageant and the hills and rivers were
        contestants —

    *

Tom is hammering the kitchen wall —

    *

What will I see out our new window but more of the same, the tiny yard
        I know?

    *

A poem should be the letter you dare not write or send —

    *

Everyone needs a manual which says

    *

how to postpone failure, flirt with it,

    *

find the hidden music, a mollusk, buried within its shell —

    *

May it not be grating and solitary as this cadenza!

    *

I am eager for the cadenza to end so I can hear the orchestra like the
        townspeople

    *

gather around the heroine and tell her she's not dead or mad —

    *

I've made a mess that will take a lifetime to clean

    *

and when I finish I will be dead

    *

and I will have lived only to clean

    *

and repair a structure light as air

    *

that comes, like fireflies or phlox, without instructions —

    *

The state I am reaching toward is depletion's sister,

    *

fullness — illusion (I smell a burning house)

    *

that the poem holds more of me than I myself contain

*

so I become the skinny tagalong, the extra

*

ghost remaining when the poem has ceased its endless revolutions

*

like a kid spilled off a merry-go-round (his head cracked open) because the
    wheel whirls too fast —

*

I dream of Dionysus every night

*

and when I wake I touch his vanishing, golden spine and remember

*

I am not alone in the world, he will chaperone me

*

through a dangerous, inexpressible country

*

pointing out the safe vistas

*

and screening my sight from the unsavory chasms —

*

Dionysus is what I've not yet found the strength to say

*

because he leaves me naked, without words

*

to ameliorate the emptiness —

*

VII

At the Memorial Garden beside the abandoned mansion

*

a purple blossom fell in my hair, only recollected

*

when I looked in the mirror, at home, and saw the blossom and threw it in the
    garbage can —

*

A man at the Memorial Garden took off his shirt and I noticed the underarm
    hair's precise

*

brushstroke

    *

and the tan-line on his upper arm,

    *

voluptuous interruption, like Violetta storming in with champagne glass

    *

to sing "Libiamo"

    *

without emphasis, without self-knowledge,

    *

not seeking beauty, just speed –

    *

I am not tubercular nor are my desires suspect

    *

as Violetta believed hers to be –

    *

I have until four o'clock to reach ecstasy

    *

and to record it – or

    *

to record it and thus reach it –

    *

Will a structure

    *

surprise me – will I

    *

be the innocent bystander who happens upon

    *

this wreck and has the power to see it as a prayer?

    *

I smell glue – my life is about to fall apart

    *

or it is just beginning

    *

because I am afraid of the space between my thoughts,

    *

afraid of ambiguity's

    *

underlying plane

    *

unstably rotating, not

    *

the root we expected when we began to dig,

*

like looking in the mirror hoping to see myself and seeing, instead,

*

a stranger asking a foolish question with his eyes alone –

*

A glance's power to undo a life of prevarication has never adequately been
     expressed –

*

How do I know when to stop

*

a thought?

*

I ask my soul and my soul usually has the right answer –

*

but how can I separate my soul from its shady surrogates?

*

The present is corroding

*

and turning out to be the original day of my life when I wrote "Slavery Is
     Aval," wrong spelling for

*

"Slavery Is Awful" – a story about my captivity

*

to a playground guard I nicknamed "Twiggy" –

*

and yet Twiggy, in her turban, made me feel solid as an anvil –

*

Twiggy said "Your mother's from Brooklyn?"

*

because Twiggy could hear I bore the scars of a Brooklyn accent

*

and Twiggy could see I was embarrassed and afraid

*

that I would waste recess

*

on a game I didn't love

*

and that I was waiting to embark on a trip to a carnival

*

that won't be as fun as advertised –

*

a Ferris wheel going haywire

*
which we want to ride but also despise and know isn't good for us
*
and Violetta, like myself, craves the silence now surrounding her
*
because the first act is over and I will not turn to the second act,
*
intermission offers me
*
a chance to comment on what just came before
*
while an anticipation as if I were about to wet my pants
*
overtakes reality and renders it false and dismissible –
*
It would be nice to write about a subject
*
such as "skull" or "my night in Damascus"
*
and fully excavate its meanings
*
but I never swerve from myself
*
which is why I spend so much time alone, snaking
*
forward using one moment as the springboard
*
for the next
*
explosion like the fountains at Villa d'Este,
*
dormant when we visited –
*
In the presence of brides
*
I in shorts and *Blue Guide* felt clumsy and contrite –
*
also my shorts were beginning to smell since I'd worn them without pause for
two weeks –
*
Don't shirk my life's obscurity, dive into it
*

rather than skim, a gnat, across its surface –
*
My life dresses me up in thought
*
like a bride doubting
*
whether she deserves such a big ceremony –
*
I am waiting for the second act to begin
*
and I am the only one with the power to put it on
*
and if only I could find
*
words other than "free" or "imprisoned"
*
to describe the mind's flight!
*
I made my eighth-graders scan a paragraph
*
from *The Old Man and the Sea* and then describe what their scansion proved –
*
One smart student said "This assignment is screwy"
*
but how could she guess I was trying to prove
*
that time is not free but bears a secret pattern
*
which, uncovered, reveals
*
mysteries of *your* personality, every beat
*
speaking your drifting secrets,
*
your feverish Pietàs –
*
Bells tinkle
*
all day as if a spirit were meditating
*
but without incantation, incense, or sacrifice, you can't know it is a
    ceremony –

*

You must take my word for it –

*

The world is so full of boredom and decorum

*

why should I add one syllable of moroseness?

*

A fine dust sifts from the blank wall where Tom removed the old window
and carved space for a new

*

three-paned casement,

*

and the word "pied" comes to mind, as if a freaked

*

flower, part violet, part cream, were announcing its twin allegiance –

*

I love the dust on the coffee-pot

*

because dust,

*

commanding, yet obedient to whim,

*

is a token of transformation –

*

I can't wait to strip off my streetclothes in the locker room and put on my
black Speedo

*

and, blind, stare at the lightbulb, through steam, and imagine I am a sailor

*

nearing port, traveling through clouds at night,

*

without companion, without compass, listening for the lone weary foghorn

*

marking the place of embarkation and return –

*

I should end with the word "return" – because if later I want to begin again

*

the word "return" will seem to have paved the way, to have licensed in
advance

*

my resumption of existence –

*

The sky now seems
*
ashen, as if the former universe hurt when it was demolished
*
and the current sky must suffer a somber tint as a consequence –
*
The question of whether I deserve ecstasy is still undecided –
*
I'm not sure my happiness has a ground
*
or whether it should be revoked, whether I should stand in judgment
*
of my calm and take it away because I discover
*
I am petty, undeserving
*
of the blanket I wrap around myself when I am five years old playing
    "king" –
*
I lack a crown
*
but reverie composes a mist
*
reminiscent of a robe –
*
Here comes a clarity so bracing and unprecedented
*
I lack a vocabulary to render it
*
unless I ask the backyard's impatiens
*
whether they are coated with grime from the kitchen wall sawed down
*
or whether their triumphant, flirty heads have shaken off the dust,
*
unwilling for the sun to see them in any apparel but their
*
own pink hoods, the color
*
of milk and blood combined –
*
I've put lead fetters on my feet

*

because I'm afraid to move forward, wanting, instead, to linger in a place I've
    never seen or named
*

until now – call it nativity or call it nothingness –
*

I've substituted a vocabulary of elation for one of despair –
*

Each is equally untrue –
*

Tomorrow or today when I rise from the pool
*

I will look back at this happiness and learn to distrust it –
*

I will regret that I ever stepped out of the shade into the fierce light
*

without querying the light and asking what business it had breaking open
    my life –
*

I call it "rapture" but that is just a name
*

for movement into the ivory
*

four o'clock light, the exact hour I began
*

to breathe –
*

The medium we are swimming in together
*

has a lovely lapping way of seeming to stand still
*

long enough for us to devise a name for it –
*

The price of registering the ebb and flow
*

is that I recognize the devil's handprint
*

as well as the rush and blur of the angel's wing –
*

It's fun to use religious language, it makes me feel
*

I am cleanly and mightily

*

looking down at a town from a great height, as if astride an equestrian statue,
*

and not condemning what I see –
*

If I see who I am too clearly, "I" may evaporate, or become
*

a baser element,
*

pebbly and bitter on the tongue –
*

When I see the word "Wayne" I think of a foursquare little boy with cowboy
boots and hat
*

and a fat round complacent face,
*

a boy riding a tricycle or a miniature fire-truck
*

or a boy dragged in a wheelbarrow past tract homes, sunshine the sickly
ochre
*

of those tinted shades that protect shoestore window exhibits from fading –
*

I've seen small, pathetic, unfashionable stores zealously
*

guard their articles from sunbleaching –
*

If you display the same goods for a full decade
*

you need to keep their hues intact –
*

VIII

When the morning's absinthe–clouded nocturne ends
*

I will have to contemplate the question of my freedom
*

of choice
*

and the quandaries that accompany any leap into the abyss –

*

Stillness has invaded my brain, as if at last I've achieved

*

separation from the space around me – at last

*

it is a dead body, without demands or depth –

*

I am not speaking solely of myself, you are included by analogy –

*

Last night I dreamt we murdered a friend

*

and a fragment of my soul –

*

She lives in my house but her backyard has

*

tea roses and the sun pours more generously into her kitchen because she is
blessed

*

with the capacity to criticize herself

*

(now Ravel's *Rapsodie Espagnole* reminds me of imaginary bygone days

*

when I loved myself without reason or reserve) –

*

We thought she was dead but

*

carted into the ambulance she closed her mouth over a thermometer

*

and her arms twitched –

*

I said, "Maybe the arms of the dead always twitch"

*

but I knew we'd not killed her completely, she was still alive –

*

Did I feel remorse as attendants wheeled her into the ambulance –

*

was I curious about her body temperature?

*

I am always interested in my own, I take it ceremoniously

*

whenever I feel a slight cold coming

*

to see if fever has arrived as threatened –

*

You may think that the woman I murdered was my mother

*

and may think me the possessor of an ugly mind

*

but aren't dreams, unlike deeds, morally neutral,

*

dream–murder

*

as distinct from actual murder as the sun from a copy of the sun?

*

Part of my cold self detests this ragged right edge

*

and longs to manicure it, like nails, or a hedge,

*

but I am bad at gardening, and the soul is not a plant –

*

I just counted the last line's syllables on my fingers

*

to see if the syllables added up to a number I found attractive,

*

a horoscope predicting good fortune,

*

but the number was rude and incorrigible, fourteen or seventeen,

*

and told no story but murder –

*

The *Rapsodie Espagnole* conveys lassitude and curiosity

*

about the identity of the speaker

*

though an orchestra is not one voice, it is a mob –

*

I must not keep any secrets from the page, even though

*

honesty, itself a pose, contains its own darkness –

*

I've jumped on my soul's trampoline too many times, it has lost elasticity –

*

I once loved a violist who knew that words

at times betray uncertainty about their fitness
*
such as these words
*
and she would say "mouth" as a code to signal
*
that a forked tongue was speaking –
*
I would rather stay silent at the moment and not tell you again about the
violist
*
I loved, who wrote on her arm with a razor –
*
I said I wasn't going to tell you and now I have,
*
stiffly, reluctant to divulge,
*
wanting to keep one romance
*
remote from the touch of these meandering lines
*
like a funicular riding higher and higher and taking the skiers to their deaths –
*
I will have to give up these asterisks,
*
trade them in for a more constricted page
*
because you would like the lines to take less space,
*
to be clothed less ostentatiously –
*
Yes, the bravado of a spacious page can irritate a reader
*
because we don't want the poet to preen –
*
A reader is not a mirror –
*
Who will tell us if we've wasted our lives
*
and is it possible in the middle of a wasted life to change
*

and stop wasting it

*

and, retroactively, to polish the already tarnished years

*

and make them seem redeemed?

*

Or is it possible to dissemble, to say, in a blind moment,

*

my life was not a waste

*

and even if secretly (God knows the difference) your life *was* wasteful

*

to delude yourself into thinking it blessed?

*

I don't know if I am wasting your time

*

or my own –

*

I don't know what *time* is and therefore can't judge if it is being wasted –

*

I've hated the organ ever since I pageturned for an organist

*

and spilled the pages over his pedals – he scowled –

*

Why was I pageturning?

*

Daydreaming through church gigs,

*

I wailed my trumpet, marking time,

*

waiting for a more pointed fate to rescue me –

*

In fourth grade I could reach above the staff

*

but by seventh my embouchure had collapsed

*

and I went slowly downhill

*

having never ascended very far –

*

Now I'm pouting, and I would lie on the floor and blame the ceiling's

*

patterns for my surfeit of spleen

*

but Tom is here to put in a new window and

*

so I'll go downstairs to say hello and thereby escape my sadness,

*

or I'll shrug my shoulders – or shiver, like the murdered girl in my dream –

*

to shake off an unsolicited ecstasy

*

that will end soon and leave me deflated and mystified –

*

My father used to shiver when Chopin's military moments unfurled –

*

and once when the *Emperor* Concerto came on the air

*

he said Beethoven was master of melody

*

which isn't true, Beethoven was master of *development* –

*

he worked to the ground his small fragments, extracting oceans

*

if you believe the ship-in-a-bottle theory of art –

*

My breathing speeds up when Chopin's Fantasy

*

bolsters nostalgia with nationalist aspirations

*

and fills the air

*

with immortality, about which I don't care a fig, and with the specificity of
   tonight,

*

when I want to look back on this morning's reverie

*

and sing along with it

*

and snort through my nostrils, tense as a horse,

*

as if trying to prove that I own the music or at least

*

have a familial relationship to the ecstasy it produces in youngish men –

*

Chopin has reached his *stretto*

*

when the octaves start marching up the Boulevard des Invalides

*

toward Napoleon's gaudy tomb, a pit I've stared into, admiring —

*

When the Chopin ends I will be less cheerful and it will be incumbent on me
to tell you about summer camp,

*

Hillbrook, when I was six and rode a horse for the first time

*

but because I don't really want to tell you about myself

*

I will put on more Chopin —

*

I am afraid of what I wrote an hour ago, as if it were the rat poison

*

New Haven Parks and Recreation Department sprayed on the orange bushes

*

in the Memorial Garden, an orange so concentrated and unconditional,

*

so beyond any preparation I had brought to the scene of its unfolding,

*

that I just stared at it and didn't tell anyone

*

what I was feeling —

*

there was no one to tell, I was alone —

*

A supplicating squirrel approached me —

*

I refused, I said "Shooo!"

*

Hatred of squirrels isn't misanthropy, but is symptomatic

*

of a distrust for living creatures

*

harbored, like most mysteries, wordlessly —

*

I should depict absolutes such as the bottle of hair tonic

*

sitting on the vanity, without thoughts,
*
enduring strong sunlight through a cracked rose window I shut for privacy's
    sake –
*
It is easier to destroy than slowly to reconstitute
*
the object of one's scorn
*
in the image of Galatea's
*
beloved face –
*
I have made metamorphosis my soul's secret specialty –
*
Though you might think me leaden,
*
changeless Wayne,
*
I seem to myself (as you must seem to yourself)
*
mercurial, I'm never certain
*
who I will have become
*
and I promise you this poem is not a direct transcription of my thought but a
    skewed
*
image, refracted by falsehood and fable –
*
When I decide at noon to stop that doesn't mean I've stopped
*
consciousness –
*
no – I plan to go on thinking for the rest of the week
*
and to record some in my journal and some in letters and to let the rest
*
spill over into phone conversations or tears –
*
I hear a buzz as if a bee were caught inside the piano's lid,
*

a sound so abrasive to the concerto's sense

*

that I will turn Tchaikovsky off before he's reached a climax

*

and put on string quartets – I think we're in the midst of Debussy

*

but I can't tell you exactly how Ravel's and Debussy's

*

musical signatures differ

*

and I must not let a prideful tone ruin the composition

*

just when it is beginning, like a custard, to set –

*

I resent the presence of *you* in today's verse –

*

who says *you* exist, are listening, are willing to be addressed?

*

Maybe you want to read this in privacy, unmolested by apostrophe –

*

This afternoon I will lose patience with myself and grow tempest-dark

*

or I will feel protected

*

as if in a car traveling toward the Grand Canyon

*

which I have never seen –

*

I no longer care if my mother,

*

a quality of the atmosphere

*

that enters my mind whether or not she's physically present,

*

reads this, because it has moved past

*

exposé into a meditative

*

mode – Reader, rescue me

*

from the impulses

*

that produce the poem in which you, saint-in-a-shrine, are enclosed!

*

Commas give me a measured tingle, as if reality were controlled and
    photographed –

*

Without commas I feel underwater and slimy –

*

If I telephone Ellis who wrote an essay on AIDS and Dracula

*

will I lose the thread of this conversation

*

or will it blossom in a new strange form,

*

without a trace of who I have been and what I have desired?

*

"I really hope I haven't done a bad deed," I just said to space –

*

my room silent now because the Ravel quartet has ended

*

though in my heart I'm confident it was Debussy, I know

*

his bittersweet eschewal of futurity –

*

Ellis wasn't home, so I missed the chance to hear my voice

*

collide with another's

*

and the Debussy turned out to have been Ravel –

*

How pristine it would be to regain innocence and live in San Francisco on a
    hill

*

with weather as boxy and bebop as Mondrian

*

rather than this sporadic, tumid life,

*

the only life I will ever know

*

and which I love, much as I regret its perpetual descent

*

into night and ambiguity – I'd rather stay aboveground where meanings

*

are clear and – unsentimental –
                    *
My poetry teacher killed herself – by noose – at an asylum –
                    *
woman to whom I never said, "You changed my life, are
                    *
changing it right now" –
                    *
Sanctity – I know its odor – invades my room
                    *
and my voice – and because I am wandering
                    *
I will return this afternoon, though I promised myself
                    *
I could stop for good at noon –
                    *
but I want to sacrifice once more, to know I've not been mistaken
                    *
and the only way to prove an experience is to repeat it –
                    *

IX

I only believe in the huge and the grandiose –
                    *
For a long time I have been striving to be natural
                    *
and only now, in this quixotic fashion, have I achieved
                    *
a semblance of sincerity –
                    *
There's no music in the background so I feel like an unaccompanied
                    *
suite – naked –
                    *
In the pool I saved an important thought to tell you:
                    *
there is no "you,"
                    *
you are the bed on which I recline and dream –

*

The question *am I deluded* will trouble me for the rest of my life –

*

It would be a joy to write a sonnet sequence about my travels

*

but first I must fly and see landscapes I can later record –

*

The sentence sighs

*

as if it were the earth and we were falling

*

again from paradise –

*

we are always falling – every time I put a word on paper

*

I am continuing the fall

*

and making it an occasion for praise and jeremiad –

*

The two – grief and celebration – often sound the same –

*

Please remove all taint from your voice, this is your last chance

*

to be natural, and this weekend if you want to look out the window

*

at the backyard you had better be passionate *right now* –

*

Ecstasy is an excrescence

*

not fastened to the experience –

*

we find it appended, like wax,

*

and can scrape it off and let the instant be shineless –

*

I hear in spatial terms

*

and now I remember what it was like to be stoned and horny and listening

*

to the Goldberg Variations on George's bed in college –

*

he a Russian prince in exile

*

and I a commoner –

*

I a budding homosexual and he

*

heterosexual and interested in LSD and mathematics –

*

Recondite friend, I never saw you naked –

*

You could call me "variations on a theme," and the theme is paranoia

*

defined as the soul's intrinsic state

*

of being split in two adversarial parties

*

trying with difficulty to reach a truce –

*

In the steam room today I saw an overeager oldster with a semi hard-on
    (semifreddo)

*

and I flatter myself that I was its apparent or sufficient cause,

*

a floating catalyst

*

among other instigations – including the room's heat and his own
    nakedness –

*

He must find display stimulating –

*

I saw the strangest sight: a woman's pump – black, scuffed,

*

propped on a mailbox, deliberately left there –

*

Of course I had a ready explanation –

*

Someone found the shoe and put it on the mailbox

*

so when the shoe's owner returns

*

she'll cry "Ah!" and claim it

*

but the shoe fit into the homeopathic poem I was reading

    *

and reminded me of the red shoes in Proust and the women's shoes

    *

in Kenneth Cole that make me gaga

    *

with envy and sad certainty that here is something (high heels) worth
      admiring and attaining –

    *

Liszt's harmonies convince the listener that she's arrived at the right party

    *

but where is the host?

    *

We see guests ranged like firing-squad victims against the wall –

    *

How happy I'd be to hear the Mephisto Waltz –

    *

I'd tap my Satanic side –

    *

This nocturne is too sleepy and pastoral, my own

    *

appassionato

    *

violences in relief against its swellings and sobbings

    *

appall me and urge me to quell my wrath

    *

against no one in particular –

    *

Writers should use their five senses, I once learned –

    *

touch, taste, smell, hearing –

    *

I sat for a few seconds dumbfounded, trying to remember the last of the
      senses: sight –

    *

Why then I will fly off to Naples in my head – Naples the sign of faded
      grandeur

    *

and seaviews – I savor houses stacked against the Bay

    *

though when I stood above Naples and looked down at said sight

    *

I saw my own ecstasy at perceiving it

*

through the scrim of my expectation that I would love it

*

which didn't diminish the pleasure

*

but made it two-tiered and diverse –

*

Later, will I murder this Tzigane and cut out its heart

*

or nurse it back to health

*

or dance on top of it and throw it in the flames like Azucena's baby in
    Trovatore?

*

O for a recording of Schumann's under-rated *Album for the Young!*

*

My life is more than a search for mood music, but while I'm at it I want to
    find lines

*

of music to match

*

the reveries waiting to shudder

*

into life – if I don't provoke a little horror I won't have

*

encouraged the mind's solitary

*

windblown particles to migrate, and to speak –

*

My mother used to get crabby in the late afternoon and, don't you know it,
    I am cranky and jittery now –

*

disappointed in my possibilities

*

as a person dedicated to expansive instants –

*

Now the carpenter is leaving which means I can strip –

*

Do any decent poets write in the nude

*

and would their nudity *while writing*

                    *
appreciably influence the poem's words?
                    *
Remember when I walked through J.C. Penney with my femmy friend,
                    *
a fellow actor, in junior high?
                    *
We bought a bag of malted-milk balls and strolled by garden tools –
                    *
lawnmowers, scythes –
                    *
That year he exposed me to Carole King's "I Feel the Earth Move" and
        Barbra Streisand's rendering
                    *
of "Where You Lead" – he was leading and I was following
                    *
straight through garden tools
                    *
toward an apotheosis outside the frame of his knowledge, or Barbra's –
                    *
The pinnacle sounded sexual from a distance but up close
                    *
I saw it was not compounded of memory
                    *
but of anticipation – and you can't remember the future
                    *
except rhetorically – O the power
                    *
of a hand-driven sentence to mow down what has not yet occurred!
                    *
Catapulting reverie used to remind me of Empedocles
                    *
staring into Etna
                    *
but now it reminds me of hippie pads and shared hygiene supplies –
                    *
the possibility of infection –
                    *
Yes, my discourse is, at root, phobic –
                    *
Inadvertently stepping on cum
                    *

in a dream's dark hotel room,
*

I was afraid I'd catch HIV through a crack in my chapped foot –
*

I pretend to be immune
*

to decorum but I, too, wish this had the graciousness
*

of chintz drapes closing –
*

I wish that I could reach
*

through language
*

toward landlocked cities beckoning –
*

Land and ocean are my favorite concepts, they make me think of differences
*

and entrapment, of voyage
*

and incarcerations I seem recently to have escaped, I,
*

no longer an enemy of the wet and the dripping,
*

fond of the sea
*

though I grew up afraid of it –
*

There can't be much difference
*

between the ground and the sky
*

though all our cosmologies depend on the distinction –
*

A wishing-well composed of dreams and dreads
*

lies at the bottom of the mind
*

and I haven't drowned in it but have some of the infernal glow,
*

a starry raiment, around me still,
*

*

If I end on a less than ecstatic note I will be doomed

*

to repeat this expenditure

*

which would be tiresome and perhaps terminal –

*

I should end on a symbolic, occult number, like twenty,

*

because I'm born on September twentieth, and Chopin

*

was twenty when he wrote the E-minor Piano Concerto –

*

I fainted last December in the bathroom –

*

sprawled on the floor until Steve found me –

*

a dramatic scene, though it happened naturally, unstaged –

*

All my life I'd wanted to faint –

*

a precise way of losing consciousness

*

or suspending it –

*

"End" is not just one moment

*

but a fluid event

*

that itself never ends –

*

not one instant of termination but a gradual

*

unveiling – only in the crudest symphonies is one absolutely sure

*

the ending is about to happen, like a wound –

*

My mother said "It's bedtime" and turned off the lights

*

and I fell asleep, dreamlessly

*

unperturbed by shadows of the future or the trees making

*

tattoos through the cantaloupe drapes

*

like Kabuki dancers tracing laden stories –

*

I'm stumped now, and that's fatal

*

so I will trick myself and say

*

this is not the end –

*

I am going to continue tomorrow –

*

I am just closing up shop temporarily so I can eat a rice cake

*

and turn on *Luisa Miller*

*

to the *a cappella* ensemble

*

at the end of Act Two Scene Two ("Ahimè, l'infranto core")

*

and await the seascape, the sunset

*

the glass of wine

*

that bubbles and deceives –

*

I believe it is burning –

*

Say something cleanly and then pack my voice away

*

and never be bothered again with this urge to speak –

*

Outside the window I hear a grackle, or two, or three –

*

Are they affiliated by birth, or love, or propinquity?

*

I wish it were two summers ago, and it will never be two summers ago –

*

I wish it were now –

*

I wish it were May 1991   –

      *

I wish I were thirty-two years old and writing

      *

a meditation on why I am alive right now here saying these things in this
      perverse

      *

choiceless fashion – at this pace and with this lack of rigor –

      *

I wish I were me

      *

sitting here abstract and aloof

      *

objecting to the rhythm of this sentence as it emerges whole from my mouth

      *

and I wish I were me about to skip downstairs and look again out the window
      to find the three

      *

or two or one grackles on the tree

      *

in my yard or the neighbor's

      *

and I will tell you it doesn't matter because property

      *

is shadowy and vanishing –

      *

The impossibility of finding a point of rest

      *

and security and soundlessness with which to end

      *

makes me feel like Abraham, obedient, slow, in love with sacrifice,

      *

about to smash Isaac, his son, to pieces –

      *

but I've already made the mistake, I've already

      *

taken some false lord at his word, and spilled the boy's blood,

      *

and nothing I can say to you will bring him back to life.